HOW TO BECOME A

a famous writer

BEFORE YOU'RE DEAD

ALSO BY ARIEL GORE

The Traveling Death and Resurrection Show

Atlas of the Human Heart

The Hip Mama Survival Guide

The Mother Trip

Whatever, Mom

YOUR WORDS IN PRINT

and

YOUR NAME IN LIGHTS

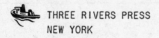

THREE RIVERS PRESS
NEW YORK

HOW TO BECOME A

a famous writer

BEFORE YOU'RE DEAD

ariel gore

Published in the United States by Three Rivers Press, an imprint of the Crown Publishing Group, a division of Random House, Inc., New York.
www.crownpublishing.com

Three Rivers Press and the Tugboat design are registered trademarks of Random House, Inc.

Grateful acknowledgment is made to Marcy Sheiner for permission to reprint "I Write in the Laundromat" by Marcy Sheiner. Reprinted by permission of the author.

Library of Congress Cataloging-in-Publication Data

Gore, Ariel
How to become a famous writer before you're dead: your words in print and your name in lights / Ariel Gore.—1st ed.
p. cm.
1. Authorship—Marketing. 2. Authorship. I. Title.

PN161.G63 2007
808'.02–dc22 2006025829

ISBN 978-0-307-34648-3

Printed in the United States of America

DESIGN BY ELINA D. NUDELMAN

10 9 8 7 6 5 4 3 2 1

First Edition

I would rather be ashes than dust! I would rather that my spark burn out in a brilliant blaze than it be stifled by dry-rot. I would rather be a superb meteor, every atom of me in magnificent glow, than a sleepy and permanent planet.

—Jack London

CONTENTS

PART TWO

Master Your Craft

PART THREE

Publish Before You're Ready

PART FOUR

Play with the Big Dogs

[illegible]

[illegible] Political [illegible]

[illegible]

[illegible]

[illegible] with [illegible]

[illegible] Acknowledgments [illegible]

[illegible]

[illegible]

[illegible] Interview with [illegible]

[illegible]

[illegible] Interview with [illegible]

[illegible] to the [illegible]

[illegible]

[illegible]

[illegible]

[illegible]

[illegible]

[illegible]

[illegible]

[illegible]

[illegible]

PREFACE

In early May of 2005, I got an e-mail from my friend and rising lit star Allison Crews:

Dear Ariel,

I need some advice from you if you're willing to give it. I am ready to start writing seriously and want advice about how to approach the publishing world. I even quit my job to do it. I am terrified but I am really fucking serious. I know nothing other than I HAVE to do this book; it's imperative, I can't stop thinking about it and haven't been able to in a really long time. Can you help? Will you be my mentor?

Would you be mine?
Could you be mine?
Won't you be my mentor?

Won't you please,
Won't you please,
Please won't you be my mentor?

xo,
Alli

"Yes, of course," I said. "I'll be your anything you want me to be." But life is life. My daughter's father had recently passed away and we went to England for the funeral. I had deadlines for a novel and a new issue of my zine. The holly tree in my backyard slowly pushed its roots into the foundation of my house. The sink overflowed with dishes. Alli planned to be in Portland the following month. We could meet then, surely. We could sip double lattes at Common Grounds and talk about the writing life and how to make ourselves famous. We could share a beer and read each other's proposals and drafts.

But we did not meet.

On June 11, a month after her e-mail to me, Allison Crews had a seizure and died at the age of twenty-three.

This book, then, is my response to Alli. It's everything I know and then some, everything I would have told her over coffee or beer if life and death hadn't gotten in the way.

HOW TO BECOME A famous writer BEFORE YOU'RE DEAD

INTRODUCTION

Every morning when I open my eyes I wonder what I can do to make myself famous. It's become my ambition, almost my raison d'etre, to burst upon the city like fireworks.

—**Coco in *Shanghai Baby* by Wei Hui**

Walt Whitman was a lit star. Gertrude Stein was a lit star. Henry Miller and Anaïs Nin were lit stars. Allen Ginsberg, Ken Kesey, and Charles Bukowski—major lit stars. Maya Angelou, Nikki Giovanni, and Dorothy Allison are all serious lit stars. Susie Bright, Erica Lopez, Dave Eggers, Michelle Tea, Inga Muscio, Wei Hui, and me—we're lit stars, too! But do you think any one of us sat around waiting for a book deal to fall out of the sky and hit us on the head? Did we pace the living room, biting our nails and wondering when the *New York Times* would declare us geniuses? Of course we didn't. We self-published, we bullied our friends into becoming agents, we climbed up onto beer-stained stages, took the mic, and before a bedraggled crowd we declared ourselves literary legends.

And the crowd believed us.

Anaïs Nin got so many writer friends to talk up her diaries, they were wildly famous years before she published a single volume. Susie Bright started the magazine *On Our Backs* with a group of friends, and "Susie Sexpert" was all the buzz before she even wrote her first book. Dave Barry began his career at a small-town newspaper. Michelle Tea founded Sister Spit and toured the country like a rock star, slamming prose on college campuses and in small-town cafés. Dave Eggers published a crazy-hilarious magazine called *Might.*

You've probably been writing for a while now. You've filled journals and bar napkins with staggering metaphors and hard-mined memories. Maybe you've gone to workshops and shared critiques. You know you're supposed to "show, don't tell" when you write, and even if you're not quite sure what that means, you can do it. You can *show.* Maybe you've bought the *Writer's Market* and sent out a few blind submissions. You've heard of people who wallpaper their bathrooms with rejection letters. This, apparently, is supposed to make you feel better. It does not make you feel better. You don't have time for rejection-letter home-improvement projects. You can't afford to sit Zazen while your cherished manuscript languishes in some nameless agent's slush pile. You've got maybe a hundred years on this planet. Less if you smoke. And you want to be a lit star, man!

Well, all right. You've got the ambition. You've got the heart and the guts. Here, then, are the secrets they'll never teach you in fancy M.F.A. programs. You'll need a bulletproof ego and a juicy humble core. You'll train yourself to write like some modern Shakespeare, certainly—a lit star's got to produce heartbreaking and dreamy prose—but you'll do more than that. You'll embrace your genius and perform your stories for crowds large and small. You'll publish zines and take to the radio waves so your name will ring exciting-familiar in your readers' ears before you've even finished your first book. And because miracles come after a lot of hard work, it's going to feel like magic when—at last—you burst upon the city like fireworks.

PART ONE

give yourself a lit star makeover

I am so hip even my errors are correct.

—Nikki Giovanni

1 WRITE

Creativity comes from trust. Trust your instincts. And never hope more than you work.

—**Rita Mae Brown**

Everybody knows it because Virginia Woolf said it: You need money and a room of your own if you're going to write. But I've written five books, edited three anthologies, published hundreds of articles and short stories, and put out thirty-five issues of my zine without either one. If I'd waited for money and a room, I'd still be an unpublished welfare mom—except they would have cut my welfare off by now. It might be nice to have money and a room (or it might be suicidally depressing—who knows?), but all you really need is a blank page, a pen, and a little bit of time.

Maybe it goes without saying that if you want to become a famous writer before you're dead, you'll have to write something. But the folks in my classes with the biggest ideas and the best publicity shots ready to grace the back covers of their best-selling novels are also usually the ones who aren't holding any paper. They've got plans, *lemme tell ya,* and their book is going to be better than yours. Too bad it's written entirely on the sheaves of their imagination.

I don't know all the reasons folks pay good money to take my classes and still don't write, but often it has to do with their own high expectations of themselves and wild notions about genius. They think stories should spring fully formed like goddesses from their Zeus-heads. They read novels by masters and imagine their own books snuggling up with the classics at the bookstore. They can't fathom the reality that all these masterpieces were once messy scrawls across ripped pages. First drafts of masterpieces are rarely recognizable as such—and good writers don't leave the price tags on their work. Inspiration comes mythic-magical, but an annoying thing happens in the transmission from inspiration to worldly draft: Things come out a little fuzzy. Introductions are clunky, transitions are awkward, dialogue sounds forced, and sensory details are wholly lacking. A writer's privilege is that she can fix it later. And then fix it again. There's magic in the first raw draft of a story, but the real alchemy happens in rewriting.

It doesn't take a world of discipline to put words to paper—plenty of writers are famously undisciplined procrastinators—but it does take a commitment bordering on obsession, and it takes some humility.

○○○

It's Thursday evening and my dreamy student walks in and takes her seat, empty-handed.

"Didn't get a chance to write anything this week?" I ask.

She shakes her head, looks down at her lap. "I didn't have time."

And I nod.

"When do *you* have time to write?" she asks.

And I answer as honestly as I can: If I'm on deadline, I write furiously. A chapter a day. One of my best writing teachers, Ms. Sarah Pollock back at Mills College, taught me that it isn't the most talented writers who are widely published, but rather the ones who meet their deadlines. So I've always met my deadlines.

Left to my own inspirations, I write in spurts and stops—sometimes every day for hours and sometimes not at all. Weeks pass. I think I'm blocked. What does that mean, "blocked"? I decide I'm empty. With some relief and some nostalgia, I think it's over—this need to put thoughts to words and words to paper. I consider other jobs, like carpentry or bartending. I romanticize more physical hobbies like weight lifting or cooking. I forget all about it. I get distracted. And then one day I wake up from a strange dream of elephants stampeding over bridges and I sit down to a blank page and see what comes of it.

That doesn't answer my student's question, of course. The answer is that I write when I can.

As a teenager, I traveled all over Asia and Europe, almost never enrolled in school, almost never punctuated my days with a regular job. I didn't have much money, so I slept in hostels, squats, train stations, and doorways. I had all the time in the world. Sometimes I sat in near-empty cafés, bored out of my mind. Aside from a cork-covered journal that took me four years to fill and an hour to burn, I wrote nothing.

I've never been more productive than I was in my early twenties. I had a baby, took a full load of college classes, worked part-time, spent a day out of every week dealing with bureaucracies at the welfare office, the financial aid office, or family court. Still, my daughter's infancy lent an urgency to my days. I wanted to be a writer. Even if I produced nothing publishable or otherwise presentable to the world, I had to write. Something. Every day. Sketches. Observations. Whatever. I wanted to be a writer, so I became one. *How?* I wrote things down.

Later, when I finished grad school and my daughter started elementary, I wrote every day from nine A.M. to one P.M. Four hours seemed a goodly chunk of time, but I kept to a leisurely pace. No mad-rushing, computer-key-banging, scribbling-across-a-blank-page-just-to-fill-it dash through the night toward the inevitable moment when the baby would wake, hungry and demanding a tit, pulling me away from the kitchen table and into the bedroom we shared, forcing me, finally, to lie down, to feed her, to fall asleep. And dream. Nine A.M. to one P.M.

Then I invited a partner to come and live with us. *Nine A.M. to one P.M.* But wouldn't it be nicer to go out to breakfast than to write? Wouldn't it be just as well to sit and talk?

I'll write nights, I decided, before I go to bed. Night: The sun sets, painting things orange. My daughter needs help with her homework. She needs to be tucked in. *Kiss me good night, Mama. Tell me another story in the dark.*

At last she's asleep. Or she's not asleep and I leave her with instructions to count porcupines. From the dark of her room to the flickering light of the living room . . . there's a trashy Lifetime movie on TV and we've got some cheap wine. My neck hurts. The chiropractor says it's because I use the wrong muscles to move my arms. *Oh, well.* Weary eyes, tired of focusing. I've seen this movie before. I take out my contacts and change into my pajamas, jot a few blurry lines across the top of a yellow legal pad. Should I get my glasses? No. *Turn out the light, dear. You can write tomorrow.*

And so it goes. There are children to be raised, money to be earned, wine to drink, movies to watch, lovers to kiss.

When do I write? I write when I can. I've learned that I work best on deadline, so I invent my own closing dates and trick myself into believing something bad will happen if I don't have, say, twelve pages by Tuesday. I write during the day when my daughter is at school. I write at night when everyone else is sleeping. I write in the morning before they get up. I write in the afternoon when my daughter is on the phone. I bought a blue velvet couch at a garage sale and put it out on the covered porch and it became my office. I've picked up the pace. If I get an hour, I can write five pages. It's nothing Kerouac would have been proud of. *Fuck Kerouac.*

I write while I'm driving. This is probably rather dangerous. Worse than being on the cell phone, really. But I try to be careful. I write in my head and then I speak it out loud so I won't forget and then I jot it down at red lights.

This is why I do not take the freeway.

I learned to write while driving when my daughter was small and her car seat provided the only respite before sleep. Later she got a plastic car and tooled around our concrete backyard muttering half-lines of poetry as she turned the wheel because she understood that this was how to drive—you mutter and then you write at red lights. I don't even look down at the notebook in my lap as I scribble, because if I do, the person behind me inevitably starts raging on his horn when the light turns green and I don't budge. I keep my eye on the signal, hoping it will stay red just a little bit longer, and I write in a shorthand that's part English, part Chinese, and part random symbolism. Arrows and circles and plus signs and ankhs and a cursive that would make my third-grade penmanship teacher weep serve as my first draft. It's pretty hard to decipher it all when I get home, but I do the best I can.

"But I don't have any time to write," my student says. And I don't ask her how it is, then, that she has time to come to class. I'm glad to have her, even empty-handed. Instead, I offer some suggestions: If you don't have time to write, stop answering the phone. Change your e-mail address. Kill your television. If you don't have a baby, have one. If you have a baby, get a sitter. If you work too much, work more. If you don't work enough, work less. If there's a problem, exaggerate it. If you're broke, go to the food bank. If you have too much money, give it away. If you're north, go south. If you're south, go north. If you don't drink, start. If you drink, sober up. If you're in school, drop out. If you're out of school, drop in. If you believe you have a year to live, imagine you have a hundred. If you believe you have a hundred years to live, imagine you only have one. If you're sane, go crazy. If you're crazy, snap out of it. If you've got a partner, break up. If you're single, find a lover! The shock of the new—shake yourself awake. There is only this moment, this night, this remembrance rolling toward you from the distant past, this blank page, this inspiration yielding itself to you. *Will you meet it?*

You don't need money and a room of your own, you need pen and paper, and my gift to you now is Marcy Sheiner's most excellent poem, "I Write in the Laundromat."

I write in the Laundromat.
I am a woman
and between wash & dry cycles
I write.

I write while the beans soak
and with children's voices in my ear.
I spell out words for scrabble
while I am writing.

I write as I drive to the office
where I type a man's letters
and when he goes to lunch
I write.

When the kids go out the door
on Saturday I write
and while the frozen dinners thaw
I write.

I write on the toilet
and in the bathtub

and when I appear to be talking
I am often writing.

I write in the Laundromat
while the kids soak
with scrabbled ears
and beans in the office
and frozen toilets
and in the car
between wash and dry.

And your words
and my words
and her words
and their words
and I am a woman
and I write in the Laundromat.

Virginia Woolf had a point with all her talk about money and a room. I catch her drift. We all need a level of emotional and practical autonomy if we're going to write. Within authoritarian relationships, the creative life becomes taboo. But here and now in this millennium, to continue to believe that we need money and a room suggests that the creative life is some kind of luxury we may never be able to afford. I reject that. My experience rejects that. I've noticed that female authors and mothers are the ones most frequently asked how we find time to write. It is assumed that men and folks without kids aren't having to make up excuses about why the dishes aren't done. But this attitude does a disservice to us all. Male or female, responsible for five children and two dogs or just for ourselves, we've all been conditioned, pressured, and bullied into believing that our creative lives are selfish nonsense. We want to be good, so we put creativity at the end of our to-do lists:

Wake up
Shower
Make breakfast
Take kids to school
Walk dogs
Do laundry
Call Dad and tell him I got a real job
Go to work
Write memos: "Enclosed please find the enclosed enclosure."
Pick up kids
Pay bills
Feed dogs
Watch evening news
Get paranoid
Go to Safeway to buy salad kits and pre-marinated chicken
Make dinner
Write novel

And then we kick ourselves because the novel isn't written. We look down at our laps and blush when our writing teacher asks us if we got a chance to write this week. Of course we didn't get a chance to write—it was the last thing on our list. We had a glass of wine with dinner.

We got sleepy. I'm going to tell you something, and it is something I want you to remember: *No one ever does the last thing on their to-do list.*

Grab a pen and paper, and if you're going to use them to write a to-do list, make sure you give yourself time to write way up there at the top.

2 DREAM

To build any creative life you need two things: dreams and action. It's true that even if you can visualize in perfect detail a published book, it ain't never going to happen without daily work. But if you can't imagine the life you desire, no amount of squirreling around is going to get you there.

All doing and no dreaming makes Ariel a dull, stressed-out busybody. And so I dream. I imagine, for example, that this book is already done. My imagination doesn't make me lazy (*Oh, yeah, I already finished that*), but it relieves me of all the stress and struggle about whether it will ever be finished. I imagine it finished. And then I work.

Imagine a few of the things you intend to write in this lifetime. Imagine the stories or the books or the plays. Imagine the *process* of writing them. Imagine late nights at the computer and sunrise inspirations. Imagine the products of your creation. Imagine the satisfaction of completion. Picture your byline in the magazine, the dog-eared books, the opening night. Close your eyes and *see* the reader on his couch turning pages. Imagine the audience sitting in the dark. Imagine your book in the library—a bridge beyond time and death.

First there was the word, it says in the Bible.

We are here to create.

But "it takes a heap of loafing to write a book," Gertrude Stein said.

It's true that planning to write a book is not writing. Telling people you are going to write a play is not writing. But alone-time dreaming and envisioning and pacing and loafing, well, that *is* a part of writing. It's a natural and important part of writing. If you write your to-do list and give yourself three hours in the morning to write and you find yourself staring off into space for the first hour, your mind empty, don't kick yourself for procrastination. Procrastination is doing the laundry and obsessing about money instead. Procrastination is surfing the Internet. Procrastination is talking on the phone. Spacing out and loafing and dreaming and waiting quietly for a bird to come to your window, ah . . . Now we are getting somewhere.

3 OBJECTIFY YOURSELF

Think you can't be a lit star because you're a teen mom or a polyester housewife? Because you're too tall or too old? In a wheelchair or in prison? Think again. It's your funkiness that makes you special, memorable . . . famous! Don't try to hide your quirks, *exaggerate* them. Other people are going to objectify you anyway. It's a lit star's job to beat them to the punch. Objectify yourself. Turn your weakness into your strength. Tell the madcap passionate stories only you can tell. Covered in baby poop and rushing to geometry class, dressed up in a furry suit and towering over your audience, running over fools who insult people with disabilities—you will be that teen mom lit star, you will be that Big Foot lit star, you will be that wheelchair lit star!

One excellent truth about literary stardom—as opposed to rock stardom or movie stardom—is that you don't have to be pretty. You can be downright funny looking. Take Stephen King. There's a weird-looking guy. Major lit star. Tortured childhood? We can work with that. Wrong side of the tracks? Excellent. Suburban wasteland? Perfect. Writers can get away with just about anything, so long as they make it part of the story.

I recently showed up tired and road-weary to do a reading at a packed bookstore in Burlington, Vermont. I staggered in, no makeup, stained sweatshirt, bad hair, sweaty and running late. The next morning's paper noted that I looked "every part the harried single mother." Perfect! It just so happened that I was reading stories about single motherhood. I looked like hell, but I was so good, the reviewer simply had to assume that my failure to find a Laundromat on my way into his barely habited state was part of the show. It *became* part of the show. I looked every part the lit star!

Make a list of everything about yourself that makes you unfit for literary glory. Surely you are too straight or too gay. You come from some godforsaken town no author ever hailed from. You were too traumatized as a kid. You had—gasp!—a happy childhood. You are over- or under-educated. Write it all down. Now write down everything about yourself that makes you the perfect literary superstar. You're a comic genius. You're a polyester housewife or a teen mom. Now string your likely and unlikely lit star credentials together and see if you can spin them into a bit of a fairy tale. Here's an example: "Ariel Gore's transformation from globetrotting teenager to the hippest of mamas reads like a movie script about a Gen X slacker following her bliss to unlikely success." Okay, so the *Utne Reader* wrote that one for me, but I couldn't have said it better myself. A shorter tag line will work, too. "Marc Acito is the gay Dave Barry." "Michele Tea is the working-class dyke who stole the heart of San Francisco." "Dave Eggers is the orphan comic genius who raised his little brother." Maybe you're the bald cowboy, the straight Marc Acito, the Prozac housewife turned homewrecker. Don't wait for other people to pigeonhole you or tell you what you are. Take your first stab at branding yourself.

4 HOW I BECAME A NOVELIST

An Interview with Marc Acito

Marc Acito, a.k.a. "the gay Dave Barry," is pretty sure that he's the secret love child of Liza Minnelli and Peter Allen. It would certainly explain his effervescent personality and fondness for prescription meds.

Originally trained as an actor, Marc studied singing in Europe and made a name for himself doing comic character roles with the Seattle Opera, Opera Ireland, and the Colorado Opera Festival. He was lauded for "his booming voice and rubber face," but Marc knew it in his heart: He was simply too eccentric to be a classical musician.

Enter *The Artist's Way,* an inspirational how-to book on reclaiming the creative life by Julia Cameron. Following Julia's instructions, Marc wrote his "morning pages" and took himself on "artist dates." Twelve weeks of creative indulgence and it hit him: He didn't want to act out somebody else's opera; he wanted to write his own damn opera! And so he was reborn as . . . a rising lit star!

He started small, writing short humor columns for a bimonthly newspaper, then syndicated the column himself. For four years, "The Gospel According to Marc" entertained readers of twenty alternative newspapers across the country.

His comic debut hardcover, *How I Paid for College: A Novel of Sex, Theft, Friendship and Musical Theater,* won the 2005 Oregon Book Award and made the American

Library Association's Top Ten Teen Book List. An Editor's Choice in the *New York Times*, it has been optioned for a film by Columbia Pictures, and is being translated into four languages Marc doesn't speak.

YOU DESCRIBE GETTING YOUR FIRST BOOK DEAL AS A CINDERELLA STORY, BUT PEOPLE FORGET THAT CINDERELLA WORKED HER BUTT OFF. CAN YOU TALK ABOUT THE WORK THAT CAME BEFORE THE MAGIC?

Selling the book was just Cinderella at the ball. I think if there's any lesson to be learned from my experience, it's the power of dreaming big and starting small. I started a writing career five years before I sold the book, taking the most mundane freelance assignments, trying to make uninteresting people sound interesting. I had no training as a journalist—I was an opera singer—but for me, one of the best things for being a writer was my training as an actor—you learn how to inhabit a character. My next book is first-person female, which is daunting, but as an actor not quite so daunting.

What I learned as a journalist and then as a columnist was how to write on deadline, how to be edited, how to market myself, and—because I wrote a humor column—how to be funny on demand. I wrote the column for *Just Out* in Oregon, starting in 2000, and then immediately started self-syndicating. The good thing about writing for small gay papers was that I could get the publisher on the phone. They are less well-insulated. Sometimes the publishers themselves would answer the phone—they were publishing out of their homes. By the time I went to sell my novel, I could say that I was syndicated in eighteen papers nationally.

In any business they say it's who you know, but that's not true—it's who knows *you*. When I went to Chuck Palahnuik's reading of *Lullaby*—an evening that changed the course of my life—I handed him a copy of his book to sign and told him my name and he said, "Oh, yeah. I know who you are. I read your column." As a result, he was able to recommend me to his agent without reading my manuscript. I mean, who has time to read a manuscript? But he was able to say, "There's this guy who writes this really funny column."

I LIKE THE STRATEGY OF PUTTING YOURSELF OUT THERE AS A COLUMNIST SO THAT YOU'RE FAMOUS ENOUGH TO SELL A BOOK WHEN THE TIME COMES. DID YOU THINK OF IT AS A STRATEGY?

Well, I wrote the column because I wanted to, but I also thought of it as a strategy. In business there's a term called a "loss leader"—you offer something cheap to get people in the store. I thought of my column that way. It gave me a platform and it gave me some credibility. That little column led to some big things. I always tell people: Write for whomever. Every two-bit periodical is a good launching pad, even the PTA newsletter. For instance, Ariel, you're somebody's mother. You might read the PTA newsletter, and maybe you'll read this little thing in there and now that writer is known by a published author.

I HEARD A RUMOR THAT YOU WROTE *HOW I PAID FOR COLLEGE* IN FIVE-MINUTE INCREMENTS. IS THAT TRUE?

Yes. It's true. Not all of it—sometimes I could carve out a few hours in the middle of the night—but I literally wrote at stoplights and between sales calls. I was working sixty hours a week at a job that I hated and then every other week writing the column and every other week drawing a comic strip. The beauty part of it is that I never had time for writer's block. There are statistics—you could probably find them if you are interested—but school athletes' grades tend to go up during their sport season because they have to monitor their time.

YOU DID THE *ARTIST'S WAY* COURSE. . . .

Yes. That's what caused me to jump track from one medium to another. When you're an opera singer, you're a thread in someone else's tapestry. I wanted to weave my own tapestry. I was thirty when I realized that.

DO YOU STILL WRITE YOUR MORNING PAGES?

No. But I DID *The Artist's Way* with a capital DID. Twelve weeks. It's wonderful. It's terribly narcissistic, totally self-absorbing, and life-changing. I don't do the morning pages anymore, but I think a lot about artists' dates and inspiration, particularly when I'm writing full-time. I get spent. The well goes dry. Your first book you've got your whole life to get ready for—after that you're on this every-couple-of-years schedule. For me, walking is golden. Or getting in water. I take really long showers. And singing, for me at least, is a palate-cleanser. I don't journal. I'm amazed at how people can blog. I'm just not that prolific. Between pimping the first book and writing the second, I can't keep up. But that's also because I write humor. I'm supposed to always be fucking funny.

WHY FIRST-PERSON PRESENT TENSE?

Every story is told by someone, and there's something so immediate about first person. When I write in third person it feels too remote. And it gets less funny.

I love present tense—again that sense of immediacy. The quality that you're there. Think of when you tell a joke: "Two guys walk into a bar . . ." Sometimes I think that with so many medias vying for attention, writers have to take their readers by the lapels and grab them.

DOES YOUR ACTING BACKGROUND MAKE DOING PUBLIC READINGS EASIER?

Yes. My readings are a musical extravaganza. I put together a ninety-minute cabaret act—it's like *Marc: The Musical*. I'm an extrovert and I was a public performer, but it's still difficult. Being a writer is one thing, but being an author is two things. You are either absolutely isolated and alone in your room with your thoughts and your words, or you're exposed to crowds of people.

DO YOU HAVE A THEME SONG FOR WHEN YOU'RE FEELING DOWN OR FRUSTRATED?

Okay, this is embarrassing because it's so very gay—but it's Barbra Streisand, "Don't Rain on My Parade."

MARC'S ASSIGNMENT

a few of my favorite things

Make a list of all your favorite books, paying particular attention to those you wish you'd written as well as those in genres you don't wish to write. Take time to analyze the list. Is the project you're working on consistent with what you love to read? If it is, what is it specifically about those books that you love? Ask the same question about those books that are very different from what you write. Are there qualities in those books you wish to embody in your own writing? The point here is to use your taste in books as a map to find your way in your own writing.

5 SEE YOURSELF AS AN ARTIST *AND* AN ENTREPRENEUR

I'll tell you about a young writer I know. She's still a teenager, but anybody who's anybody in the literary community in this town knows her name. Soon they'll know her name in bigger cities, too. I predict a book contract by age twenty. Her prose streams tormented and inspired, but I could never make such a prediction based solely on art. The writing comes first and last, but there's a whole world in between. Good storytelling opens the doors, but you've got to be an entrepreneur to get into the living room, and this girl isn't afraid to get herself invited in—she's a traveling saleswoman selling a story. She contacts agents, holds her own with editors. She's not pushy—she's rather shy, in fact—but she's determined. Slam the door in her face and she'll move on, undaunted. *Next house.* She takes both rejection and praise gracefully. If one thing doesn't work, she tries another. She reads at open mics and invites published authors she thinks will enjoy her work and help her to expand her territory. I mean, the girl sends thank-you notes. She's crafted a plot for her career and it has a happy ending.

Maybe she's the best young writer I know and maybe she isn't. It doesn't matter. She understands something about America most artists imagine they'll be able to skate over because they're so damn talented. What matters are the classic qualities of an entrepreneur—the traits and attitudes that predict success. *Entrepreneur:* a risk-taker who has the skills and initiative to establish a business and accept profit or loss. An entrepreneur is . . .

Competitive
Self-confident
Driven to succeed
Willing to work long hours
Open to criticism and rejection
Able to see the world as a system
And willing to take care of her physical health

Most of us aren't born with all these qualities, but we can cultivate them. We can work them like muscles, pushing ourselves a little bit harder each day until we've got the strength we need to use our vision and take over the world.

Writing is an art and a craft, but with the right kind of work, it can also become a job and a business. Because there aren't that many employers looking to hire lit stars, most of us have to become our own employers, creating our own jobs and cultivating our own audiences.

In the beginning, you probably won't get paid for much of what you write, but as you start putting your work out into the world, you'll begin the networking and marketing necessary to turn your art into your career. As you develop as a writer, it's fair and right that you get paid for what you do.

Get over any hang-ups you may have about trading words for money.

When I was about ten years old, bored and broke, I decided to do a series of abstract paintings and hang them in the garage. An art show! I'd sell each piece for a few cents or dollars depending on its size and complexity. I did the paintings, copied the best one onto a flyer, and went door-to-door with the news of my opening. One pinch-faced neighbor who lived in a three-story house all by herself took one look at my little flyer and shook her head. "I don't believe in paying for art," she said.

Back home, I whined to my mother, "You aren't supposed to sell art for money."

"Who told you that?" my mother, a working artist, demanded.

I whimpered the name of the guilty neighbor.

"Well, she's wrong," my mother said. "She told you that because she's a greedy witch who doesn't think people should be paid for their work." And then she turned on her Birkenstock heels and marched out the door to give our poor neighbor a talking-to.

Written stories are no different from visual art. When you make a poem and give it to another person, you are providing him with something that has the power to sustain him. You could just as easily be making him a sandwich. It's a creation of your generous heart, but it is also a product. You are the brand; the poem is the product. This frame of mind needn't change the way you create your written work, but it should be put to use when you bring that work into the marketplace.

Start paying attention to the literary products you buy and consume. What draws you to the books and zines you end up bringing home? How are they marketed to you? Steal the strategies that work for other writers and publishers, abandon them if they don't work for you, and try something else. Don't take it personally when an editor doesn't want to publish your short story or a neighbor doesn't want to come to your opening. Just try something new. You'll always be improving your craft and your product, but you'll learn to improve your marketing and promotion, too. Practice ambition and hard work. Learn to take both compliments and critiques with a "thank you." Every day, choose to do something emboldening. Every day, do one thing you'd rather procrastinate. Begin to see the lit world as a system, and figure out how to work it.

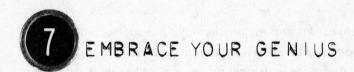

6 DON'T TELL ME YOU'RE TOO OLD

Video hasn't killed the lit star yet. James Michener was forty when he published *Tales of the South Pacific.* Frank McCourt was a sixty-six-year-old retired schoolteacher when *Angela's Ashes* came out. Maya Angelou published her debut memoir, *I Know Why the Caged Bird Sings,* at forty-two. Fannie Flagg was forty-three when *Fried Green Tomatoes at the Whistlestop Café* came out. And Mark Haddon wowed the lit world at age forty with *The Curious Incident of the Dog in the Nighttime.* Everything you lack in adolescent glow is fulfilled with life experience. Youth can be an asset if you're not afraid to sell it, but your every scar and wrinkle are assets, too. So don't tell me you're too old.

7 EMBRACE YOUR GENIUS

I think Haruki Murakami is a god among lit stars, but my own attempts to write Japanese sci-fi surrealism from the perspective of an underemployed Tokyoite have fallen flat. This is because, due to a cosmic error of incarnation, I am not Haruki Murakami. I was born two decades later on the opposite edge of the Pacific Rim to hippie artists. A different fault line ran through my birthplace.

I've drafted stories in which I am abducted from my Tokyo high-rise condo by psychic prostitute space-women, and I've had fun doing it, but, alas, I've had to abandon these projects. Imitation is never as good as the real thing. The world doesn't need another Haruki Murakami. It already has one.

However! The world might need me. And it might need you. Because, as I learned from my California hippies, neither of us would be here, dear reader, if the world didn't need us.

You have a unique and delicious genius to share. You see this vibrant and vulnerable planet in your own strange way. You draw connections that make you wonder if you've lost your mind. Your fears are specific, and alien to me. We're human kin, you and me and Murakami—when we dig deep enough into our own individual wells, we reach the same universal stream—but the places we're digging from, they're different.

❍❍❍

Genius: *In ancient mythology, a supernatural being appointed to guide a person through life.*

What does your genius look like? What does it sound like? Do you know? Or is she sitting there in the corner neglected because you've been busy chasing Murakami's or Whitman's or Doris Lessing's genius? Do you want to be the next Flannery O'Connor? Or do you want to be (your name here)________—perhaps widely compared to Flannery O'Connor and heavily influenced by Edwidge Danticat, but a true original all the same?

Please choose the latter.

Embrace your own genius.

Yeah, that neglected one over there.

The sweet thing about a genius is that she doesn't seem to hold grudges. She's like the kid on the playground you kicked last week—jump too fast and she might retreat, but sit down quietly and offer to share your Tofurkey sandwich and she'll cheer up immediately. She'll take a bite. "Whatdoyawanna play?"

8 GET YOUR HEART SMASHED, BUT JUST ONCE OR TWICE

> A crucial ingredient for the formation of a novelist—romantic humiliation and heartbreak. The unhappy childhood gives you the tools of observation. Unrequited crushes, romantic despair, a few memorable breakups, will give you something to write about, an understanding of grief. No prospect of heartbreak in sight? I can provide phone numbers upon request.
>
> —**Jennifer Weiner**

When bad things happen to writers, there's always the silver glimmer of a good story. *Damn*, we think when we're face-down on the rain-wet pavement, nose broken and bleeding, coughing betrayal. *This is gonna make a great story.*

The toxic weasels in our lives teach us about plotting and scheming. The sweet-talking jerks who play rugby with our hearts expand our compassion for characters both living and imagined. Don't let them break your spirits—you need your spirit scarred and whole—but every time you expose yourself to annihilation, you come that much closer to grasping all that is indestructible in a soulful human being.

When everything goes to hell, write. If nothing readable comes of it, write. Don't write for perfect clarity now. Write not to forget. Entertain the possibility that grief and heartbreak are cleverly disguised gifts from a benevolent universe that knows beyond knowing that you're just the writer who can turn pain into a powerful and healing elixir.

9 HOW TO STAY FLASHPROOF

An Interview with Julia Alvarez

When asked what made her a writer, Julia Alvarez points to her emigration to New York as a child. Although born in the city, she spent the first ten years of her life in her parents' native Dominican Republic. When she got back to New York, she hardly understood the language. "I had to pay close attention to each word—great training for a writer."

From a young age, she knew what she wanted to do, but in the sixties and seventies, stories that focused on Latino characters were considered "of ethnic interest only," so she made a living as a migrant teacher with Poets in the Schools programs in Kentucky, Delaware, and North Carolina, and then as a creative writing professor in Massachusetts, Illinois, and Vermont. In 1991 she published the "little novel" that would earn her tenure—but *How the Garcia Girls Lost Their Accents* became a *New York Times* Notable Book and instant classic and catapulted her career in a new direction. Since then, she's published poetry collections, children's and young-adult books, political memoirs, and four other novels, including *¡Yo!* and *Saving the World*.

Julia gave up her tenured post at Middlebury College in 1998 but has stayed on as a writer-in-residence, advising students and teaching occasional courses. She and husband Bill Eichner started a sustainable farm/literacy center on the slopes of Pico Duarte in the Dominican Republic. You can order their Alta Gracia coffee from cafealtagracia.com.

YOU'VE TALKED ABOUT COMING FROM A CULTURE IN WHICH WOMEN ARE NOT ENCOURAGED TO SPEAK UP. I KNOW A LOT OF WRITERS STRUGGLE WITH QUESTIONS AROUND "WHAT IS MY STORY TO TELL?" AND FAMILIAL OR CULTURAL SILENCES-INCLUDING THE SILENCES AND SECRETS NECESSARY FOR SURVIVAL. HOW DO YOU DIFFERENTIATE BETWEEN THE URGE TOWARD SILENCE THAT'S REALLY SHUTTING UP AND BEING COMPLICIT IN OUR OWN

OPPRESSION AND THE URGE TOWARD SILENCE THAT MIGHT ACTUALLY BE A LOVING INSTINCT TO PROTECT OUR RELATIONSHIPS AND OUR VULNERABLE ALLIES?

I don't think I have any answers to that. You sort of find your way as you go along. In general I believe the truth will set you free. You have to show the complexity of people. A lot of times you find that what people want you to write is flat and not very interesting. They want you to write "the official story," and that's not your job as a writer. But sometimes your loyalties to them come into a struggle with your desire to tell the truth. You have to take care of your *familia* and your community.

You can always write what you want and then decide what to publish. Maybe you will delete things. But you want to be sure it's more about being a decent human being than emotional cowardice.

I think it's problematic when you come from a marginalized community. The stories you hold and the stories that bind you together—when you tell those stories it feels like a kind of betrayal, so that's complicated. You have to weigh it out for yourself. I, personally, don't think we need to hunker down in our ethnic bunkers. It's like the Roman playwright Terence said, "I am human, nothing human is alien to me." I hold that faith and belief. But if I had an answer to your question, then I would be suspect. I've often gone ahead and published what I thought was a fair, complicated, and rich version of my story.

HOW DID YOU WRITE YOUR FIRST BOOK? YOU WERE A SOMEWHAT NOMADIC PERSON AND HAD TO WORK. HOW DID YOU DO IT WITHOUT MONEY AND A ROOM OF YOUR OWN?

How the Garcia Girls Lost Their Accents wasn't published until I was forty-one, but I majored in creative writing in college—actually I majored in English, because you couldn't major in creative writing then—but I was focused that I wanted to be a writer. To earn a living, mostly I did Poets in the Schools, but I took any job that would at least give me a little time to write. I forgot there was a price—all the uprooting and moving around—so there were many, many years in which I was just trying to earn a living. By the time *Garcia Girls* came out and did very well, I was writing because I had to. I was writing because I was passionate about it.

I thought of *Garcia Girls* as my tenure book. People said, "You'll never get tenure unless you have a book." So, ironically, I thought of *Garcia Girls* as my little novel that would get me tenure, and it ended up being the book that made me a writer who does some teaching on the side. It was a long struggle, but it made me not lose my focus. It built a kind of grit. It made me skeptical of the book biz—the biz and the buzz. I do the promotion because it's the new world—you can't sell a book unless you peddle it, too. Just to get the people to know it's there involves this whole publicity machine.

With all the focus on very young writers, you start to feel like, *Oh my gosh, I'm past the age because I'm thirty.* I feel like the focus can become so much trying to make it and become famous, but when you're young and lionized, it can be difficult to keep writing. There's so much pressure, and when you're young, that can be damaging. Of course, it depends on your personality. For some writers, celebrity appeals to them. It totally doesn't appeal to me. I'm so glad I'm in Vermont. You can lose sight of what it's all about. You can start believing in your own celebrity. The books are what it's about. Spike Lee said the only way to be flashproof is to keep doing the work. So you have to remember that it's about the work.

DO YOU FIND IT MORE OR LESS CHALLENGING TO COME OUT AND BE VULNERABLE IN YOUR WORK, KNOWING THAT YOU CAN, IF YOU CHOOSE, PUBLISH ANYTHING YOU LIKE?

Beginners mind. Each new book—you have to learn how to write it. Robert Frost said, "No surprise in the writer, no surprise in the reader." If you're not growing as a writer, it's not going to be interesting to you. Your craft develops, but you're also having to learn to write *this* book, so those skills apply, but you have to cover new ground.

HOW HAS YOUR WRITING PROCESS CHANGED SINCE YOU'VE HAD MORE TIME?

There's *never* enough time. I gave up my tenure so I would have more time, but now I'm doing all the stuff that comes with being an elder in the profession. My students write books and ask me to blurb them. Blurbing can take up all your discretionary reading time. My husband, Bill, says, "Why don't you just say no?" But I say, "Who are they going to ask?" I went to my teachers and mentors when I was starting out. It's like in the Dominican Republic—we have a farm and a literacy program there—and the people, whenever they have a problem, they come to us. Bill says, "We're already doing all of this work." But I say, "Who else are they going to go to? They don't have insurance." So there is all of this that comes with being the older generation. Somebody called reading all the NEA grant applications "literary jury duty." People will ask me, "Will you have your assistant send me this or that?" I say, "I'm my assistant." And people have so much access to me with seven degrees of separation.

YEAH, WHEN I WAS LOOKING FOR CONTACT INFORMATION, A FRIEND SAID, "HER HUSBAND IS MY EYE DOCTOR!"

And that's okay. Now, I hardly ever blurb books except for my students. But if you're going to have some power, you can do some good. It's part of being a decent human being. Still, you have to stay focused as a writer. Mothers know this. How can you be a good enough mother and still carve out some time for yourself? Those balances are tricky—there are no rules. You have to chart your own way. It's like when my students ask me how to begin a story. I want to give them a string in the labyrinth, but there are no rules. They come up to me and they tell me the plot of their story and they say, "What do you think?" Well, if a student came up to me and said, "I want to write a story about a man who wakes up one morning and he's a cockroach," I'd say, "It will never work!"

DO YOU HAVE ANY FURTHER ADVICE FOR DEVELOPING WRITERS?

Tell them to read. A lot of them don't read, and they should.

JULIA'S ASSIGNMENT

finger exercises

You have to develop the habit of writing. If I had to wake up every morning and decide if I felt like writing, nine times out of ten I wouldn't feel like it. You're not going to choose to write every day. Once you've chosen it passionately in your heart as what you want, you have to make a habit of it. If you're a dancer and you don't do your floor exercises for a few weeks and then you go out and try to dance, you're going to pull a muscle. It's the same with writing. You have to practice. The worst thing you can do is tell yourself you're going to write something good and important. Just tell yourself you're going to practice. You can do finger exercises. Read some haikus by Basho and go out and do a series of haikus, little snapshots of the landscape. Henry James said a writer is someone on whom nothing is lost. These little haikus get you to really develop opening all of your senses. And with something small, we can look at how the words are working. You don't have to stick to the traditional three-seven-three structure, but if it's something small, you can really focus. Emily Dickinson said, "There are no approximate words in a poem." So use these finger exercises to develop your agility.

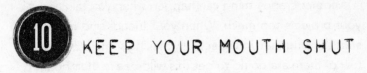

10 KEEP YOUR MOUTH SHUT

> When one is trying to do something beyond his known powers it is useless to seek the approval of friends. Friends are at their best in moments of defeat.
>
> —**Henry Miller**

Don't talk about the thing you're writing. It's not as if you have to be secretive. It's not going to hurt anything to say, "I've been working on some fiction," or "I'm writing an episode of *The West Wing,*" or "I'm doing a book about rare birds." The problem is then come the follow-up questions. You need to come up with some short answers, because there are some seriously lit star–killing things that can happen when you start talking in specifics about your work.

First off, a story just doesn't *like* being talked about. The more often you describe the plot of your novel-in-progress to a friend over cocktails, the less likely it will ever get written down. You'll dilute it, scatter the good bits, get tired of hearing the same scene. Hell, you've told it enough times, why bother writing it at all?

Have you ever heard a professional writer describe in detail every twist and turn of the book she's working on right now? No, you haven't. This is because professional writers know that stories can get scared off very easily. We want to protect them.

Another crappy thing can happen when you talk about your projects too much. When your friends and relations start thinking that you're actually making some progress, a few of them are going to get this wild bee in their bonnet and decide that it's their goddess-given job to knock you off your high horse and clue you in to "reality." Maybe you *are* on some high and mighty horse and out of touch with reality. I don't know. But more likely, you're just writing a story. You're doing something beyond your known powers, and this seems to bother some folks. They'll say things like, "Yeah, well, it's very difficult to get books published these days." Or "Humph, I know a woman who's been working on a novel for *thirty* years." Even if you've already got one novel under your belt, they'll sigh and say, "I've heard that second novels are career-killers."

Do not subject yourself to this nonsense. Either you'll internalize what these stormy-weather friends say and let it feed your natural fear, or you'll grow to hate them. And it's not that they're bad people—they'll be perfectly supportive if you break a leg or get dumped by the love of your life—it's just that they've got a wild bee in their bonnet. So keep quiet. Or tell them you're writing about colonics. That oughta shut them up.

11 CHOOSE A GOOD VICE

It is a great paradox and a great injustice that writers write because we fear death and want to leave something indestructible in our wake and, at the same time, are drawn to all the things that kill: whiskey and cigarettes, unprotected sex and deep-fried burritos.

It's true that you can get away with drinking and smoking and sunbathing when you're in your teens and twenties, and it's true that rock stars are free to die at twenty-nine, but a lit star needs a long life.

Choose your vice carefully. Long walks and yoga classes, Vietnamese salad rolls, flower essences, and purified fizzy water. Either that or you'd better start writing a heck of a lot faster.

12 BE JUST AS CRAZY AS YOU ARE

You know those eyes people look at you with when they've decided that you're crazy? If you don't know what I'm talking about, that's all right. Insanity is no prerequisite for the creative life. I've met many a fine sane writer. I've met many a lit star who takes his meds. Don't go crazy because you think it'll make you a better writer. Your work doesn't need you tragic or depressed. But if you know the eyes I'm talking about, listen: Of all the jobs they said you couldn't have because you were too whacked in the head, your response time off, your perceptions misaligned with the consensus reality—well, author wasn't one of them. You can be a whacked author. There's an undeniable link between madness and genius. You can be just as crazy as you are. Go and rent a copy of the movie *An Angel at My Table*. It's like *Chariots of Fire* for writers. Accept your madness. As long as you're not hurting anyone, you have my full permission to be weird. You'll have to learn to promote yourself and talk business when business time comes, but you can wander off into artist mode more often than not, and when you're there you can be exactly as misresponsive as you are.

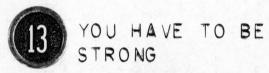

13 YOU HAVE TO BE STRONG

An Imagined Interview with Haruki Murakami

There comes a time in every lit star's career when he doesn't have to give interviews anymore. In fact, he doesn't have to do anything he doesn't want to. Rebels and hermits, every writer gets to decide for himself when that time has come, but the decision might not be so difficult once you've written a dozen international bestsellers and they've been translated into thirty-four languages, once you've won every literary honor in Japan and your latest tome has just been named a top book of the year by the *New York Times.*

Suffice it to say, I did not land an interview with the elusive Haruki Murakami, Japan's most popular and influential novelist. I shed a few tears over my failure, but then it hit me: I don't have to meet Murakami in the dense world. I can travel to that surrealistic jazz club on the Pacific, where UFOs hover, women disappear, and eels rain down from the sky. There, I can buy Murakami a beer and we can sit down and shoot the shit while we're waiting for the sushi train.

COME HERE OFTEN?

I said no interviews.

I KNOW, BUT WE'RE NOT REALLY HERE.

Okay. As long as we're clear that I'm either saying these things or I'm not. No guarantees either way.

WE'RE CLEAR.

Very well, then.

WHEN DID YOU BECOME A WRITER?

I didn't write anything until I was in my early thirties. It was a spring morning in the 1970s. I was watching a baseball game, lying in the bleachers and drinking a beer. I got the idea I could write and I started work on the book that would become *Hear the Wind Sing*—part of *The Trilogy of the Rat* with *Pinball 1973* and *A Wild Sheep Chase.*

IT MUST HAVE BEEN A PRETTY BORING BASEBALL GAME.

It was no ordinary baseball game.

I GUESS NOT. WHAT'S YOUR WRITING SCHEDULE LIKE THESE DAYS?

To write *Kafka on the Shore,* I woke up every morning at four A.M.

MONDAY THROUGH FRIDAY?

Weekends included. I wrote for five hours and then, at nine A.M., I went for a run. Afternoons, I browsed the record stores. Then I went swimming or I played a game of squash. In bed by nine P.M. Seven hours' sleep. I did this for a hundred and eighty days and then I had a draft. It's a big book. I rested for a month, then I rewrote for two months, rested for another month, and then rewrote for a month.

I HEAR YOU RUN MARATHONS, TOO.

You have to endure and labor every day to write. You have to concentrate. That's the most important ingredient for a writer. And so I train every day. Physical power is essential. Many authors don't respect that. They drink too much and they smoke too much. I don't criticize them, but to me strength is critical. People say "He's not a writer" because I run and swim every day.

SURELY NO ONE SAYS "HE'S NOT A WRITER" ANYMORE.

Listen, I was an underground writer. I had a small following in Japan—what in America you would call a cult following. I got some attention and I did all the talk shows, but still, it was a reasonable following. I liked that. In 1987 *Norwegian Wood* came out. That book was a challenge for me, and fun to write, but it sold millions of copies in Japan alone. That book ruined my reputation.

THAT WAS YOUR ONLY REALIST NOVEL, AND NOT MY FAVORITE. ANYWAY. SORRY ABOUT YOUR REPUTATION.

(Murakami nods into his beer.)

YOU SEEM LIKE SUCH A DOWN-TO-EARTH AND SELF-CONTAINED GUY. WHERE DOES THE DARK SURREALISM IN SO MUCH OF YOUR WORK COME FROM?

I haven't read a great deal of Jung, but I know he writes about that, the subconscious. Usually it starts with an image. I have a particular image in mind and I suspect there's something deeper in it, so I follow it. I don't know where a story is going any more than I know what's around the corner—if I knew where it was going, it wouldn't be any fun—but I follow it the way I follow a dream. Sometimes it's a dream all my own, and sometimes I enter a universal dream, but I don't analyze it. I don't pick apart the symbolism. I find the riddles, not the solutions to the riddles. Often the power of a story, like the power of a good dream, is that I myself do not know what it means.

MANY OF YOUR CHARACTERS SEEM TO STRUGGLE WITH THE PROBLEM-WITH WANTING TO LIVE IN A DREAMWORLD AND WANTING, AT THE SAME TIME, TO LIVE IN THE DENSE WORLD WHERE "ALARM CLOCKS RING IN THE MORNING." IT SEEMS TO ME THAT YOUR CHARACTERS ULTIMATELY HAVE TO MAKE A CHOICE BETWEEN THE TWO WORLDS. ISN'T THERE A WAY TO LIVE IN BOTH WORLDS?

If you are an artist, yes, you can live in both worlds. You can inhabit the subconscious world and the world where alarm clocks ring at four A.M., but you have to be strong. The pull of realism and the pull of madness are equally stunning. You have to be very strong.

HARUKI'S ASSIGNMENT

anything mundane

I meet many people who say, "I've had so many interesting and exciting experiences in my life, I could write novels about them." I myself have not had many exciting experiences. The beauty of a short story is that you can test anything—a piece of conversation, a dream, a haunting memory, something overheard in a restaurant, anything mundane or resonant at all. Select a small and ordinary thing to test. Do not decide that you will write a great story from this fragment. Simply follow it in a kind of self-exploration.

14 FIGHT FOR YOUR TIME

My family respects the fact that I work at home. Really, they do. It's just that, well, "since you're going to be home anyway, can you put that load in the dryer?"

"Sure."

"And, oh, the dogs need to be walked at noon."

"Okay."

"And, oh, I almost forgot. The cable guy is coming over between nine and one."

"Right."

My friends respect the fact that I work at home. I'm sure they do. It's just that, well, "I know you're working, but is there *any* way you can take my cat to the vet? I can't get the time off and she's *super* sick."

"I really can't. . . ."

"Thanks so much, Ariel. You're a lifesaver."

I don't know, maybe if I had an office job people would call me all day and ask me to run out and do things for them, too. But somehow I doubt it. No one ever asks me to take time off for them when I have to teach. Folks respect the fact that I might get in trouble from a boss or disappoint my students. But when I'm my own boss and don't have a designated space outside the home to call "my office," it's a constant battle to get taken seriously. For me, it's usually a losing battle.

I respect the fact that I work at home. At least I think I do. But it'll just take a minute to put that load in the dryer. And of course I can take the dogs for a walk at noon. The cable guy won't take but a few minutes of my time, will he? I'll need a break by then, anyway. And the cat, well, she's *super* sick? I don't want a dead cat on my conscience. I guess I can. . . .

It's Saturday morning and I'm writing this from a secret location in Portland. I've told my family and friends that I've left town, but really I'm just in a friend's living room. She's in Nicaragua for the month and I've scored the key from the caretaker. I don't think she'll mind. But if anyone knew how close I was, the phone would be ringing. Seeing as they think I'm an hour away, they'll only call on me in real emergencies.

I might just as well be on the Oregon coast, but this way I've saved myself the hotel bill and the long drive.

I shouldn't encourage you to lie to your family like I do, so I don't have any real advice on this one. I can only say that if you find you have to battle the people in your life for the time and space to work, you're not alone. When you're not making any money from your stories, it's near-impossible to get folks to understand that you're working. But even when you're supporting a family with your articles and books and zines, that very family will feel compelled to interrupt you every fifteen seconds until you give up and get a job at Starbucks.

15 ONLY CHANGE YOUR NAME IF YOU HAVE TO

> If you really want to hurt your parents and you don't have nerve enough to be homosexual, the least you can do is go into the arts.
>
> —**Kurt Vonnegut**

Young writers always want to make up some fabulous pseudonym—Adonis Rockefeller or Evita Alameda—but what's really wrong with your name?

Ariel Gore: It starts out melodic, then takes a bit of a swan dive. Goths always like it, but other people want to know if I'm related to Al. I got my first name late. Three months old and folks were still calling me "baby." Ariel came from Ariel Durant, a woman, but my parents wanted to be sure I'd sound androgynous on paper. "I didn't foresee feminism," my mother claims. Apparently she also did not foresee the Disney version of *The Little Mermaid.* When I was in elementary school, the only other people named Ariel were Jewish boys. Now it's as girlie as Jennifer.

So, Ariel Gore is my given name, but I wasn't always proud to use it. I submitted my first manuscript to Random House, HarperCollins, and Rand McNally under the name Crystal Harmony. I'm not sure why I chose Crystal Harmony, exactly. I was six years old. My kindergarten classmates were already trying to hide their counterculture pedigree. Moonlight, the girl who sat next to me, had changed her name to Jill in September, but I, apparently, wanted to highlight my Summer of Love conception. All three publishing houses rejected my book, *Shark in the Park*, but imagine if the thing had gotten published! Imagine if it had, in fact, received wide acclaim and become somewhat of a classic of shark literature. I'd be stuck with Crystal Harmony. It's bad form to change your name midcareer, after all. The only lit star I can think of who's done it successfully is LeRio Jones/Amiri Baraka. There must be a handful of others, but I'm sure part of the reason I can't think of them is that they went and changed their name on me. Imagine if Judy Blume suddenly dropped her first husband's last name and came out with a novel by Judy Sussman. *Judy who?*

When it came time for me to publish my first article when I was in college, I had to think about it: What would I call myself? Growing up, I'd gotten used to Ariel, but for a while I'd swapped my bio-dad's name, Gore, for my stepdad's name, Duryea. Still, Ariel Gore is what I easily answered to. My bio-dad is a weird duck, but he's my bio-dad. We both have the same tendency to stare off into space before saying something inappropriate. Duryea felt borrowed—and anyway, it caused people to call me Ariel Derrière.

If you've got any doubts when you start publishing, your given name will do just fine. Keep it real. But there are a few perfectly good reasons to change your name. Maybe you were born the wrong gender and your parents didn't have the forethought to name you something androgynous like Pat or Ariel. Maybe your name is taken—the lit world can only handle one "Amy Tan" or "Stephen King." My sister, a singer, curses the day my parents thought "Leslie Gore" would be a good idea. "*The* Lesley Gore?!" folks of a certain generation always ask. So, yes, if your parents were doofuses and named you John Grisham or Banana Yoshimito, you'll have to go fish.

Or maybe your name is too common to Google. That can be a problem. "James Smith" brings up more than a million references on Internet search engines, and MariaPerez.com is taken by a six-year-old who lives near Madrid. When folks want to buy your book, they might end up with an invitation to little Maria's birthday party.

Perhaps you have a very unusual name, but there are several warrants out for your arrest. Publishing under "John Doe" might stall them for a while.

Or maybe your name represents a past or a lineage you won't ever want to reclaim: owners, rapists, colonists. By all means, if you need to disown an illegitimate ancestry, find yourself a new name.

But please remember: A pseudonym is as permanent as a tattoo. Michelle Tea's second-choice pen name was Michelle Rage. Might have gotten kind of embarrassing when she wasn't so pissed off anymore. If you write an even modestly successful book, your ex-wife and coworkers will find out about it. Regardless. If you really want to hurt your parents, the pen-name-authored book won't quite do the trick. And you may live to be a hundred—that's a lot of years to be answering to Crystal Harmony.

16 DEVELOP A SUPERHERO ALTER EGO

I learned a few things as a teenage single mom:

1. The world is not your oyster—a lot of people would rather shame you than help you out.
2. You don't need those people. And . . .
3. When the emotional stakes are high and the task at hand is near-impossible, you must develop a superhero alter ego.

I'd like to take credit for all my fantabulous and amazing accomplishments, but it's only ethical that I let you in on my little secret: I work hard, but it's my superhero alter ego who pulls the last-minute all-nighters, convinces the electric company to turn the lights back on without payment, takes the calls from my kid's vice principal.

And all these lessons have come in handy in my quest for literary stardom.

In the world of creative output, too, a lot of folks would rather cut you down than build you up. You don't need them. But you will need a superhero alter ego.

Most of us can't march our vulnerable Zen poet-souls out into the world of query letters and interviews and self-promotion unprepared. If an author gains any power or fame in this business, she usually starts surrounding herself with agents and publicists, assistants and handlers—superheroes, really—but most of us can't afford a staff right away. We've got to learn what young broke single moms and other marginalized folks already know . . . and that's how to develop and call upon an inner superhero.

See, a superhero doesn't take things personally, she doesn't waste time falling apart, and she isn't bound by the earthly laws of time and limited possibility. She's uniquely qualified for mothering, and for the show business side of writing.

When I was twenty-seven, a big-city newspaper called me "conservative America's worst nightmare." Just last month I read that I'd single-handedly changed the culture of parenting and what it means to be a mother in America. Ha! Good work, eh? Yep, I've been noted for my feats of courage and recognized as a woman with abilities beyond those of any normal human. I'd take credit if credit was due, but I'm just like the next girl. Unarmored, I can be oversensitive—even weepy. Unarmored, I care what people think. The fear of being laughed at keeps me from my bravery. Unarmored, I can make art. But I can't always take that art out into the marketplace.

My superhero alter ego writes the book proposals, reads the rejection letters, meets the crazy-tight deadlines, and tours twenty cities in eleven days.

I can't tell you my superhero's secret name or describe her fancy pink costume in too much detail—that's secret info—but if you get lucky, you just might see her flying past your window at the speed of words. There she is now, scaling a publishing house high-rise. She can perform impossible feats, change minds, move cash, clear the way for little human me.

And she can do something else, too. If you are pure of heart and want to be a famous writer for all the right unselfish reasons, then she can, through these pages, transmit to you the very superpowers you will need to accomplish your task.

When I'm trying to do something beyond my known powers and I feel wobbly or fear failure, I snap my magic gesture and my superhero alter ego emerges.

When a bout of low mama-self-esteem comes rumbling on the horizon like a thunderstorm, I repeat after Alli Crews: "Girls like me have raised presidents. We've raised messiahs and musicians, writers and settlers. Girls like me won't compromise and we won't fail." And my superhero alter ego takes control.

When money is tight, I chant the chant lit star Inga Muscio taught me: "I am a money magnet. Money flows naturally and easily into my life. Money is sexually attracted to me! Money stays up at night, thinking about me. . . ." And my superhero alter ego invisibly flies off to commandeer some cash and deposit it in my mailbox by morning.

What you are trying to do may not be humanly possibly. But that never stopped a teenage single mom—or a famous writer, for that matter.

17 WATCH OUT FOR STALKERS AND WANNABES

Dear Jennifer Blowdryer,

Is it okay if I steal your thoughts about wannabes for a chapter ranting against people who steal?

Thanks,
Ariel

Hey Ariel,

I'm flattered to be mentioned and quoted.

Yours,
Jennifer Blowdryer

Wannabes and stalkers are shadow artists, empathetic characters who don't yet have the courage or self-possession to embrace their own genius, but to the rising lit star, they are dangerous vampires and must be avoided. Writer and rock star Jennifer Blowdryer first turned me on to the fact that all creative people meet their wannabe. She calls them Eves, from that Bette Davis movie *All About Eve*. "At some point in your trendy life, somebody will want to be you. Perhaps their youth was not tortured enough, or they were tortured in the wrong way, and they are not enjoying your modest success," Jennifer warns. "These people will compliment you winningly, and that will progress quickly to shadowing you. It's kind of nice to have a flattering little shadow around, isn't it? But watch out. It's not just that they want to become you, but that they don't want there to *be* a you anymore. Ironic, isn't it? But so are most human machinations."

The startling thing about Eves is that you don't have to be particularly famous to attract one. An Eve won't talk to a "nobody," but she'll talk to anyone she thinks is about to become a somebody.

As soon as you start making a minor name for yourself as a lit star, your Eve will appear. You can spot her—or him!—in an otherwise nurturing creative community because she's the one not doing any of her own work. In fact, you'll have the sinking feeling that she's plagiarizing *your* work. If you call her on it, she'll say, "This is what creativity is all about, a give-and-take of artistic ideas." And on a certain level you agree, so you try to ignore the fact that Eve seems to be doing all the taking and none of the giving. Then she starts doing her hair like yours. And "Hey, Eve, what are you doing out here in my recycling?"

Busted and scared, she'll start talking shit about you to your friends and editors. She'll get bold, and instead of just stealing a few lines, she'll steal a whole poem and then accuse you of plagiarizing it to begin with. Folks will ask you why you do your hair like Eve's. You'll start muttering about people being out to get you and everyone will call you paranoid. Eve will win the American Book Award with a punched-up version of the manuscript she found in your recycling, and pretty soon you'll be a bitter drunk living under the bridge.

You must cut ties with these shadow artists as soon as you recognize them as such. When folks borrow your thoughts, ideas, and words, they are supposed to ask you first (see above e-mail to Jennifer Blowdryer), and then they are supposed to give you appropriate credit. As Jennifer says, "Just get that Eve out of your apartment. The friends who believed her version of you are useless anyway, and your Eve will fall apart, no longer able to suckle the organism she hoped to feed off and devour: you."

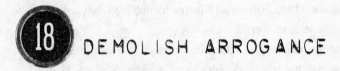

18 DEMOLISH ARROGANCE

> They're fancy talkers about themselves, writers. If I had to give young writers advice, I would say don't listen to writers talk about writing or themselves.
>
> —**Lillian Hellman**

Most writers have bad credit. A lot of us don't make enough money to pay the rent on a studio apartment over the railroad tracks. We dress like slobs. Some of us don't even brush our hair. Much of what we write is neither revolutionary nor inspiring. We lack social skills. Why, then, are writers so freaking snooty?

Early in the evening at a recent book awards ceremony, I was perplexed as to why everyone was looking at my tits. I mean, my tits are not considered particularly eye-catching in most circles, but everyone who approached me took a good look before they smiled up at me like they might like to be my friend. Later, after the awards had been handed out, I grabbed a few tortilla chips from the snack table, picked up a glass of wine, and attempted to continue my mingling. But, alas, now people looked at my tits and then didn't look up with a smile. They turned on their heels, unimpressed. Had I spilled salsa on my shirt? I looked down, and then I saw it: my name tag.

People wanted to see Who I Was before they decided whether or not to be cool. At the beginning of the evening, I'd been a finalist for the book award. Now I was just an also-ran. Folks had bigger fish to fry. They wanted to befriend a shinier lit star.

I looked across the room at some of the winners. They threw their heads back and laughed and winked at one another and snubbed the poor suckers who were checking out their tits. They were the real literati now. *Ting, ting.*

This is truly the most embarrassing thing about the writing world. Arrogance grows like mold. As a member of the next lit star generation, you have a revolutionary opportunity: to rid the lit world of this stinky, toxic green muck!

Your genius is unique, glorious as a freight train at sunrise, but here's the catch: So is everyone else's. If you're in this to get people to look at your tits, invest in a diamond-studded Miracle Bra instead. And don't check out people's name tags before you decide whether or not to smile.

Arrogance is not talking to people unless you think they are better than you. Arrogance is not talking to people unless *they* think you are better than them. Arrogance causes people to stab their friends in the back and, contrary to the arrogant one's goals, causes their friends to think they are idiots.

As you begin to convince people in your neighborhood and around the world that you're the next Ernest Hemingway, you may be tempted to fall for your own scam. A few published stories, and people will start treating you like you're something special. This is sometimes because people are arrogant themselves. More often, it's because they're socially awkward and don't know how to talk to strangers who happen to be writers. It is *not* because you are better or smarter or more talented than they are. If you start acting like a bighead, no one will like you and no one will want to support you. You'll get all weird and neurotic because you'll secretly know that you're just a little speck of dust in the vast and swirling universe, and now you'll have to worry about getting found out and unmasked and all the things arrogant people stay up at night worrying about. And then you *will* get found out and unmasked and all the things arrogant people stay up at night worrying about because you have not been nice. If all that's not bad enough, arrogance will actually damage your ability to write. Arrogant people, many of whom started out as talented youngsters who got too much attention for their minor accomplishments, lose the ability to tell the truth. By age thirty they're writing like politicians, defending themselves like they stole the election. That's because they did steal the election. The word *arrogance* comes from the verb "to arrogate," meaning to assume, usurp, seize, and take over like some crazy colonist. And nobody likes a crazy colonist.

Here's the wacky paradox: Arrogance is born of a deep-seated sense of inadequacy. You think you are a loser, so you set about trying to convince the world (and by extension your father) that you're all right.

Enough, already.

Buy yourself a cake and have the baker write your name on it and then write RULES. As in: ARIEL GORE RULES. Eat your cake. You are a genius superstar in a world of genius superstars. Now get over yourself.

19 ASK MAGNIFICENT METEOR

Rising Lit Star asks: M.F.A. in creative writing or journalism school?

Magnificent Meteor reveals: You don't need a degree to be a writer. If you don't have kids or other huge time-consuming responsibilities, consider going to school for something other than writing—major in something wacky you've always wanted to know about. Or take a job at a small-town paper. But if you do have a lot of other life responsibilities, going to an undergraduate or graduate creative writing or journalism program will give you time to focus seriously on your writing. The degree itself doesn't matter that much. You're buying time to hone your craft. So do you want to buy M.F.A. time or journalism school time? It's apples and oranges. A journalism career—even if brief—can be a great launch into the lit world, but you have to at least *sort of* like reporting. You have to get off on the adrenaline rush of a bomb threat. In journalism school (or at a small newspaper), you'll learn to write on deadline, you'll get great story ideas as you transcribe the daily police log, and you'll begin to get your name and your work out into the world. An M.F.A. program is going to be more literary arts-focused and often less career-focused—a lot of small writing workshops—but it may also lead to connections with established lit stars who can help you down the road. In my senior year of college I realized I couldn't possibly enter the paid workforce full-time, so I applied to both kinds of programs and got in. I chose journalism school because it was cheaper and I was already about fifty thousand dollars in debt. (I'm all for student loans, but there's a limit.) Journalism school made me insane because of the lack of focus on more creative writing, but it sure taught me how to write on deadline. Also, both degrees are considered "definitive," meaning that you can teach at the college level—good work if you can find it.

Rising Lit Star asks: When can I call myself a writer? Do I have to be published to be a real writer? If you could let me know before my high-school reunion on Saturday, I'd appreciate it.

Magnificent Meteor reveals: You can call yourself a writer and hold your head high whenever you start writing. No publication required. But beware the dumb reactions of former classmates. When people ask me what I do, I tell them I sell T-shirts on the Internet.

Rising Lit Star asks: Was there a time when you didn't think you were going to make it as a writer? What helped you through that period?

Magnificent Meteor reveals: The chances I'm going to make it as a writer are still very slim. Good thing I don't have any other marketable skills or I might get distracted. In the meantime, I listen to one of my theme songs, "Prove Yourself" by Joan Armatrading. I think I'll put it on right now.

Rising Lit Star asks: Do I have to read everything from ancient to modern to all the schlock in the journals? Worse yet, do I have to understand it? Jeez, what if I'm a slow reader?

Magnificent Meteor evades: I'm going to let Garrison Keillor field this one. Garrison says, "Ignorance of other writers' work keeps me from discouragement and I am less well-read than the average bus driver." Read what you like.

Rising Lit Star asks: How do I do it all—work full-time, raise my son, have a relationship, have non-work/adult life interests, relax, and find something to write about? How?

Magnificent Meteor reveals: I accept poverty, have only a part-time day job, raise my kid, don't pay enough attention to my partner, let the house get messy, don't have much of a non-work/adult life, don't relax, and drink a lot of coffee. When you're looking for a day job to support your writing work, you want something that gives you a lot of space-out time and some writing time. You want a boring job. Being a receptionist or a clerk at a slow business will work. Maybe a night watchman. Alternately, you can do something that uses a completely different part of your spirit than writing—construction and carpentry come to mind. This way you'll still have some wordsmithing energy at the end of the day. If you spend eight hours doing tech writing, or anything at a computer, you may find it difficult to write during your off-hours. Consider: changing your day job, reducing your work hours, carving out a twenty-minute space within each day or two hours a week that's your writing time regardless of your job or other responsibilities, finding another creative parent to trade child care with, and making a pact that this time will only be used for writing or creatively self-nurturing solo goof-off endeavors.

Rising Lit Star asks: How and when do you begin to formally set aside time and space for writing? And I don't mean in a way that just becomes another procrastination, like, oh, let me design my perfect writing studio and what color paint will I have in there?

Magnificent Meteor reveals: Do it now. But you're right—don't worry about the size or appearance of any physical space you may have. Barbara Kingsolver says she wrote her first book in a closet. What you need to do is formally set aside time and space in your psyche for writing.

Rising Lit Star asks: I've heard that I can claim writing workshops, conferences, research books, etc., on my taxes. I've also heard that if I don't make money after three years, my writing will be considered a "hobby" and nondeductible. Is this true? 'Cause I really want to go to the Maui Writers Conference and write it off!

Magnificent Meteor reveals: Yes, you're starting a small business as a self-employed author, so you can write off the purchase price of this very book. And yes, if your small business loses money consistently, the IRS will call you on it. If there's no income after three or five years, you'll have to stop claiming your writing as a business. Are you a capitalist or a hobbyist? Even if your writing career gets stamped "hobby," whenever you *do* start making money, you can restart your small business and write stuff off again. So if you have the money, go to the Maui Writers Conference and drink a Mai Tai for me. GO! Write it off. Why do you think they have that conference in Maui?

PART TWO

master your craft

I think I did pretty well, considering I started out with nothing but a bunch of blank paper.

—**Steve Martin**

20 DISCOVER YOUR LINEAGE

> I learned that you should feel when writing, not like Lord Byron on a mountain top, but like a child stringing beads in kindergarten—happy, absorbed and quietly putting one bead on after another.
>
> —**Brenda Ueland**

You must know that it is a writer's job to love the world. And you must know that writing is a lineage art, like kung fu. The novice studies under the master, perfecting one form and then the next, until eventually—and ever so respectfully—the novice kicks the master's ass.

Mercifully, literary kung fu doesn't require any actual physical contact. Living teachers may be helpful, but as writers, most of our masters will never even know we bowed to them.

You can become a student of Djuna Barnes or Haruki Murakami any day of the week by going down to your local independent bookstore and shelling out $12.95 for a copy of *A Night Among Horses* or *A Wild Sheep Chase*. Some teachers recommend copying out by hand each word of your master's entire book. A few pages will suffice, but by doing this you will read the entire work with new eyes and new ears. You will unlock the mystery of your master's magic. You'll peel away the paint and the plaster to discover the secret architecture that holds their stories up.

You must write the thing you most want to read. I used to think I'd be a poet because I thought it would be easier. Poets don't have to finish their sentences. But I soon realized that if I didn't live to read poetry, I could never write the kind of poems that would sustain others. I live to read surreligious novels and the rare self-help book that's actually helpful. So this is what I try to write.

As you study your masters' work, do not cower under their excellence. Remember that they, too, started out with a bunch of blank paper. Know that they, too, wrote messy and embarrassing sentences and drafts. The luxurious thing about writing—unlike spinal surgery—is that you don't have to get it right the first time. Anaïs Nin told herself, "Write a book, Anaïs. Begin anywhere." And that's where you shall begin: Anywhere. Pen to paper. Your superhero alter ego can know that you'll publish, but your sensitive writer-soul needs to be assured that it's perfectly acceptable to scribble numskulled nonsense no one will ever see.

I've done my best and worst writing by promising myself I'd never show it to anyone. Alone with the glow of my computer screen, I can be passionately outrageous and nakedly dorky. I'll decide later which is which. Maybe I'll publish both. Maybe neither.

When I have my students do freewrites in class, there are always lines they'll edit out later. But there's a coarseness and a truth they might never come to if they sat around waiting for just the right turn of phrase. In the dash to fill a page, the magic begins. Shimmering details and startling dialogue come more easily to some than to others. The rest of us can learn. We can write and rewrite. The only thing we need going in is the courage to love the world.

21 PRACTICE

God knows I've done enough crap in my life to grow a few flowers.

—**Dustin Hoffman**

Before I get too far, I should warn you that there aren't any magic formulas when it comes to craft. No writer is going to be able to hand you a secret map to literary mastery. It takes practice. You already know that. Even more mechanical endeavors—like dental care or driving—take practice. Everything takes practice. First attempts are frustrating. Hand a kid her first toothbrush and she's more likely to stick it up her nose than in her mouth. Sit her behind a steering wheel and she'll accelerate and brake abruptly, just missing your neighbor's Bentley. It's not because she doesn't have any talent. It's because she doesn't have any experience. Everything looks so much easier than it actually is. When I watch Olympic speed skaters, I always wish there was a "constant" skating in the far right lane, illustrating the average human's ability to hurtle himself around an ice rink. When I'm watching four world champions at once, it's hard to remember that most of us would fall on our butts about a tenth of a second after the gun goes off. It's hard to remember, too, the daily training it took for even the last-place skater to get so bad-ass. So, no, you're probably not going to read these few chapters and then take pen to paper and out-write Kafka. If you're going to be a lit star, you're going to have to train. You're going to have to practice. And you're going to have to read—not everything that's ever been written, but the books you are drawn to. I'll share with you the most common mistakes I see among my students, and I'll let you in on a few tricks, but that universal magic formula will remain elusive. Even Kafka wrote in the dark.

22 STORIES ARE LIKE FERAL KITTENS

An Interview with Ursula K. Le Guin

Ursula K. Le Guin hardly needs an introduction. From her *Earthsea Quartet,* which has sold millions of copies and been translated into sixteen languages, to her succulent version of Lao Tzu's *Tao Te Ching,* her work has earned the intensely private writer a good window seat on the classic American writer's train. Three of her books have been finalists for the American Book Award and the Pulitzer Prize, and she's snagged a National Book Award, five Hugo Awards, five Nebula Awards, a Pushcart Prize, and plenty more.

The daughter of a professor and an author, she grew up in a redwood house in Berkeley, studied French and Italian literature, married a man who never questioned her right to write (her advice to young writers: "If you can't marry money, at least don't marry envy"), and raised three kids. "The idea that you need an ivory tower to write in," she notes on her Web site, "that if you have babies you can't have books, that artists are somehow exempt from the dirty work of life—rubbish."

In a rejection letter for her best-selling novel *The Left Hand of Darkness,* an editor complained that "the book is so endlessly complicated by details of reference and information, the interim legends become so much of a nuisance despite their relevance, that the very action of the story seems to be to become hopelessly bogged down and the book, eventually, unreadable." If you ever need cheering up, read the whole thing at ursulakleguin.com.

THE REJECTION LETTER YOU HAVE ON YOUR WEB SITE FOR *THE LEFT HAND OF DARKNESS* IS GORGEOUSLY RIDICULOUS! BUT WHAT DO YOU DO WITH SOMETHING LIKE THAT WHEN YOU'RE EARLY IN YOUR PUBLISHING CAREER? A LOT OF WRITERS WOULD READ THAT AND DECIDE TO GO INTO CONSTRUCTION OR LANDSCAPING INSTEAD.

I wrote *The Left Hand of Darkness* when I was twenty-eight or twenty-nine. I had been sending out fiction for years, and getting some of it published for about three years. It was my first "big" novel—the three before it had been fairly short and much more conventional. I sold it myself to Terry Carr at Ace Books as a paperback, but I thought it ought really to be a hardcover, so I sent it to the agent Virginia Kidd. She jumped at it, took me on, and soon sold the book to Walker.

The letter on my Web site actually came to her, not to me, and being a very smart agent, she didn't show it to me for years—till we could laugh at it. But if I had received it myself, it wouldn't have stopped me from sending the book to another publisher. I had taken quite a lot of rejections by then—nothing but for about seven years. Experience in rejection doesn't stop it from hurting, but it helps you just dig in and go on trying.

I THINK YOU CAN BE A GOOD REALIST OR NONFICTION WRITER BY SIMPLY MASTERING THE CRAFT, BUT YOU TAKE EVERYTHING A FEW STEPS FURTHER IN YOUR FANTASY STORIES. CAN YOU TALK ABOUT WHERE YOU GO-PSYCHICALLY-TO WRITE FANTASY/PROPHETIC FICTION?

"Simply mastering the craft"? This is simple? I've been at it for sixty years, and it ain't got simple yet.

That's one reason why I wrote *Steering the Craft*—because people think it's easy.

I don't know how to answer the main part of your question; I get your drift, but I don't know what to say. Where do I go to write a story? I don't. I just sit here, waiting and waiting and waiting till the story begins to come to me. Then I sit very, very, very still and try not to scare it off. If I grab at it, it might run under the sofa and hide, or escape entirely. Stories are like feral kittens. You have to be very patient and careful and quiet and put out little bits of chicken on the floor.

Now, trying to respond to your distinctions:

I don't do prophecy. Praise, lament, description, yes; prophecy, no.

Science fiction—well, realism has to do with stuff that might really have happened, and sf is about stuff that might possibly happen but hasn't yet. So I think of sf as a kind of realism, with more of the doors open.

Fantasy is something else. All the doors are open, and the windows—in fact, there may not be any walls. Fantasy is in one way or another about the impossible. Writing fantasy, you have nothing but your craft—the whole thing is made out of words. The person to read on this subject is Tolkien, in his essay "On Fairy Tales." Therefore the consistency, the coherence with itself, of the world you're making up and the story you're telling, is absolutely essential. You can't fake it.

OKAY-HA!-SORRY ABOUT THAT QUESTION-WAY TO MUDDLE THINGS UP RIGHT FROM THE GET-GO. ANYWAY . . . A FEW MORE?

Sure. But when you print this, you have to quote your whole question, not just my answer, right?

I WAS HOPING TO CLEAN IT UP A LITTLE BIT TO MAKE MYSELF SOUND SMARTER, BUT I'LL PRINT THE WHOLE DANG THING IF YOU WANT ME TO. ANYWAY. HOW DO YOU STAY STEADY/STAY VIABLE IN A LITERARY MARKET THAT IS SUPPOSEDLY ALWAYS CHANGING? IF YOU'RE GOING TO SAY THAT YOU CAN'T THINK ABOUT THAT AT ALL WHEN YOU'RE WORKING, THEN MY QUESTION WOULD BE *HOW* DO YOU NOT THINK ABOUT IT? THERE MUST BE PRESSURE EVEN ON A FAMOUS GAL LIKE YOURSELF.

Ohhhh yeah. There is pressure. And "famous" is relative. J. K. Rowling I am not.

But the fact is, you already know it, Ariel—you said, You can't think about it while you're working.

You can think about it some while you're *not* working—while you're between stories, between books, whatever. Sitting waiting for the feral kitten to come back out from under the couch. You can think, *What if I tried . . .* Like: *What if I wrote some science fiction?* That was me, thinking, in 1964. *There's a market for short stories, there are sf magazines—what if I tried that?* It was true in '64, it's still true.

Just a few years ago my agent said, "I wish you'd write a young-adult novel again. They're so easy to sell right now!" First I thought, *Oh, I can't do that, I'm too old to write for adolescents, I don't know what kids are into these days.* But then I thought, *Fantasy? In fantasy everybody's the same age.* So that got me started on *Gifts* and the books that have followed it. I am so grateful to her for saying that!

Let your mind roam, is all I can say. To stay steady, don't worry about staying steady. . . .

As for "not thinking about it while you're working"—well, you have to be really, really interested in the story you're telling. And that takes care of it. You aren't thinking about anything but that—where is the story going?

WHEN I'VE SEEN YOU AT EVENTS OR ON THE STREET, YOU SEEM LIKE YOU ARE MINDING YOUR OWN BEESWAX AND NOT TRYING TO DRAW TOO MUCH ATTENTION TO YOURSELF. WAS THERE A TIME WHEN YOU WERE MORE OF A PUBLICITY HOUND? SOMETIMES IT SEEMS LIKE A WRITER HAS TO PUT ON A MONKEY SUIT TO GET ANY ATTENTION AROUND HERE.

I'm very shy, and a major introvert. I love living here in Portland because people let you mind your own beeswax. But I am also a secret ham, so I love doing readings, performance pieces. You have to find the balance that is right for you. A writer who likes personal attention and enjoys being in public should go for it! Why not? A writer who doesn't like personal attention should stick her nose into her work and never ever feel she has to put on a monkey suit. But for introverts and extroverts both—reading or talking to a bunch of readers can be a really great experience. It's very scary the first few times, but then most of us find we love it and are rewarded by it, if not by sales, then by human contact.

ANY ADVICE ON HOW TO BECOME A FAMOUS WRITER BEFORE YOU'RE DEAD? OR AT LEAST ONE MAKING A LIVING?

Write your heart out. Go for broke.

Submit your work for publication, methodically.

And don't quit.

Ever.

URSULA'S ASSIGNMENT

without adjective or adverb

Write a page of whatever kind of narrative you write—fiction or non—without any adjectives or adverbs. You can also take a few pages of narrative you've already written and remove all the adjectives and adverbs, rewriting the sentences as necessary. There's more about this in my book *Steering the Craft*, where I call the exercise "Purity." I do think it's the single scariest and most useful exercise I know.

23 RUSH IT

You can write a book in a month. It might not be a great book. It might not be the draft of the book you're going to publish. But you can write a book in a month. I should know—I've done it.

Conventional wisdom says that it takes two to ten years to finish a book. That figure has held true for me, but getting started can be such drudgery. All those blank pages make my knees itch. If I've got a *draft*—175 or 200 pages—well, now, that's something I can work with. Rewriting is easy. I can fix just about anything. I can smooth out transitions. I can go back and flesh out a character I've described only as birdlike. I can add dialogue that better identifies a character's class. I can get a handle on an unwieldy structure.

If getting started is your problem, too, why not tear recklessly through that first draft? Write a book in a month!

Every year, thousands of writers participate in National Novel Writing Month—NaNoWriMo to the attention-deficit participants. They begin writing on November 1 with the goal of churning out a fifty-thousand-word novel by midnight on the thirtieth. That's about seventeen hundred words a day if you're counting, and NaNoWriMo writers are counting. Seven pages a day. The goal here: quantity, not quality.

Last year, more than forty thousand future lit stars signed up to write the Great Frantic Novel. An impressive six thousand crossed the finish line. Sure, they probably wrote a lot of crap, but crap can be a good thing. By pushing yourself to *just write,* you give yourself permission to make mistakes, to take risks, to worry about editing and perfecting later, to write on the fly, to simply create, to let go. On Halloween you were someone with a vague dream of authorship. In one kamikaze month, you're a novelist. You'll never again have to wonder if you can do it.

Of course, you can draft a book in any month you like. I drafted one in June based on NaNoWriMo's philosophy, but if you can wait till November, you'll have the comfort of knowing that thousands of other writers all over the world are typing away with you. *Listen.* You can almost hear the frenzied *tap tap tapping.* Writers meet throughout the month—in person and online—to encourage and commiserate. And at midnight on the thirtieth, even if they know they can't pay their rent in the morning, they party like it's Y2K.

24 LISTEN

Every murderer is probably somebody's old friend.

—**Agatha Christie**

I adore books, but I'm not a good reader. I'm terribly slow and easily distracted. A book really has to grab me by the throat and drag me in. I didn't read my first book until I was in the fourth grade. Folks were starting to worry. "Is that one not so bright?" I'm sure if I'd come of age a few decades later, I'd have been diagnosed with this or that, but these were the seventies and I was free to be you and me. I graduated from college with honors and went to grad school, but I'm still not particularly well-read. The prospect of taking the GRE subject test in literature terrifies me away from highbrow academic pursuits.

I'm not a good talker, either. I've gotten better, but for long periods in my life I simply did not speak. When I decided to sign up for my first journalism class in college, my stepdad bristled: "You're not pushy enough to be a reporter." But as I started quietly reporting, I learned I had a talent more valuable than quick reading or extroversion: I knew how to listen. Why hadn't I noticed that before? Storytellers and crazies had always been drawn to me. They sensed that I'd be patient with them, and they were right. They could get a whole lot of words in edgewise.

Tell me a story. I like nothing more.

I haven't heard all the stories they tell you in the classics of modern and ancient literature, but I've interviewed Athabaskan grandmothers and Richmond, California, teens. I've profiled welfare fathers and traveling veterinarians. I've listened to mothers who've lost their only children to gun violence and I've had a word with Ursula K. Le Guin. I've heard stories from wealthy businessmen who've watched their mansions burn in swift-moving fires and from street people who've mastered the intricacies of the recycling business.

On the first day of Journalism 101, Sarah Pollock said that it was a reporter's job to give voice to the voiceless. You don't need to be pushy to do that. And in the process, all of these supposedly "voiceless" people will gift you with the only education a writer needs. They'll tell you how things are going in *their* lives. They'll give you stories humble and dramatic. They'll show you that the human condition, even when it appears tragic, is a mystical thing.

I spent years studying journalism, but I didn't end up having any newspaper career to speak of. The newsrooms of late-twentieth-century America weren't particularly friendly to single moms. Still, I consider myself a journalist.

If you're an expert reader and an eloquent talker,

you've got plenty on me, but learn to be a good listener, too. All the characters you'll ever need live and breathe here and now. They speak in dialects you can only guess at in your messy first drafts. They have a story to tell the world.

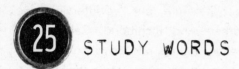

25 STUDY WORDS

English is a language of immigration, emigration, occupation, wars, and wandering. There are histories in every word—long journeys and hidden meanings. We've carried hard-edged working-class phrases from Anglo-Saxon, floral and earnest formalities from Latin. We whisper Arabic and Swahili, mingle Creole with Southern dialect. Study the etymology of your favorite words—they've traveled through many mouths and many pens.

When your characters speak, notice the way they carry their social and economic class, political education, and ancestry in their chosen vocabularies. Read my words, then read the spaces between them. Can you tell that I'm more Latin than Germanic? More Irish than Hispanic? Can you tell I never completed high school? And that I have a graduate degree? Do you know without knowing that my people valued education over income, art over niceties? Do you smell a bleeding heart?

Profane is Latin.
Hooligan is Irish.

Stoicism and *tragedy* and *pornography* are Greek.

Jazz is African.

Adobe comes from Egyptian via Coptic,
Arabic, and Spanish.

Sequoia is Cherokee.

Tulip is Persian.

Cider is Hebrew. So is *Armageddon.*

Emerald is Semitic.

Assassin and *coffee* and *magazine* are Arabic.

Meander is Turkish.

Spinster is Middle English.

Bad comes from an old English word
meaning homosexual.

Dough is Indo-European.

Demarcation is Spanish. So is *siesta.*

Bungalow is Bengali.

Lynch is white American.

Buccaneer and *cayenne* are Tupi.

Tabby comes from Iraq.

Sideburns are named for a Civil War general
called Burnside.

Mandarin is Sanskrit.

Custard is Anglo-Norman.

Sodomy is French. So are *harlot* and *chivalry.*

Flannel is Welsh.

Thug is Hindi.

Dirt and *ditch* and *crook* are Norse.

Decoy is Dutch.

Aspirin is German. So are *superman* and *Neanderthal.*

Bamboo is Malay.

And *passion* comes from the Latin verb meaning "to suffer."

26 DON'T SAY *PLETHORA*

I am hereby retiring the word *plethora.* Don't ever use it. No one ever told you they ate a plethora of food at their family Thanksgiving fiasco in Pasadena. No one ever got shot with a plethora of bullets in the parking lot of your local Super Burger. So how come every amateur essay writer in the world finds a way to sneak the word into otherwise passable prose? What does *plethora* mean, anyway? In amateur essay-usage, it just means "a whole buncha," but it sounds like some internal organ malfunction. That's because it also means you've got too much blood in your circulatory system. It's a yucky bodily condition.

The word *myriad* is slightly more melodic than *plethora.* It's a noun: *a myriad of bees.* Or an adjective: *myriad bees.* That's a lot of bees. A swarm of them buzzing toward you. But were you ever sitting at a bar sipping a Pabst Blue Ribbon and telling a friend about the myriad of bees that almost attacked you? Of course you weren't. You'll find the word *myriad* in plenty of literary classics, but no one ever says *myriad* at the bar. Through overuse, the word has lost its meaning. Perhaps there will come a time when we can reintroduce *myriad* into the English language—

perhaps in our grandchildren's lifetimes—but for now it's dead tired and needs to rest.

While I'm banning words, please don't look up *said* in your thesaurus. If you give each of your characters a strong and distinct voice, you won't have to attribute their every quote. When you do have to attribute their quotes, don't tell me your character "exclaimed," "stated," or "replied." When in doubt, just use *said.* That's all. Maybe they "answered." They certainly did not "retort." You can use *said* more than you think. Five times in a page won't bother anyone. It's one of those words that takes a while before it starts sounding repetitive. If you feel like you're using *said* too much, and you're tempted to tell me that your character "revealed" something when, in fact, she revealed nothing, find another way to attribute your quote:

Sam rubbed his eyes. "I'm tired."

We know Sam was the one saying "I'm tired" because you've got him rubbing his eyes in the same paragraph, and you've avoided this dud:

"I'm tired," Sam uttered sleepily.

Speaking of *sleepily,* don't use it unless you have to. I like my adverbs as much as the next guy, but so many writers use them unconsciously that we're in danger of all adverbs starting to sound like *plethora.* Adverbs are so easy, so addictive. Pretty soon you'll have characters "replying angrily" and "blushing shyly." Maybe you can get away with those for stage directions, but if you're writing prose, an adverb is usually a sign of laziness. You need another double espresso. What do you want the actor to do with your adverbial stage directions? Show us *that.* When you find an adverb in your story draft, you've probably found an opportunity to slow down and actually describe something in your character's body language.

Unlearn the linguistic jags you were taught that written work required. You didn't become a writer because you wanted to tell me that your brother "retorted angrily." You became a writer because you needed to show me the veins bulging from his neck, or how the wood of the door frame felt against your skull the night you went crazy. Tell me *that* story.

27 CONFESSIONS OF AN OUTCAST WRITER

An Interview with Floyd Salas

Novelist/boxer Floyd Salas says, "All considerations of language, of ideas, of symbols and metaphors serve only one function: to convey the soul of a living being to the soul of other living beings and in that process break us out of our isolation and loneliness and put us in touch with the universal spirit."

I'll drink to that.

Floyd's first novel, 1967's *Tattoo the Wicked Cross,* became a classic of modern prison literature. His other books include *What Now My Love, Lay My Body on the Line, State of Emergency,* the memoir *Buffalo Nickel,* and a book of poetry, *Color My Living Heart.* He's the recipient of all kinds of fellowships and awards—from the National Endowment for the Arts, the California Arts Council, the Rockefeller Foundation, and many others. In 2003 he landed a gig writing for the NBC miniseries *Kingpin.* Not bad for an old guy who claims he's done "not very much" to promote his career. Dedicated more to freedom than to commercial success, Floyd is his own kind of lit star, living and breathing artistic rebellion against the literary establishment, but don't be fooled: This old writer produces some one hundred poems a year, always seems to be working on at least one novel, has mentored thousands of young writers, and is a frequent speaker at conferences and political events. Well into his seventies, he is remembered for his legendary street fights in urban California, where he lives with Claire Ortalda—his editor, lover, partner, and friend of twenty-three years. Claire typed the answers to these questions, so it's "her mind straining my mind before it reaches your mind. That's a three-way threat."

To find out more and get copies of his books, click to www.floydsalas.com.

I TOOK A WRITING CLASS FROM YOU WHEN I WAS FIFTEEN. I THINK I GOT A C. BUT I REMEMBER YOU SAID THERE WAS ONLY ONE STORY: EROS VERSUS DEATH. I DOODLED EROS ON A TIGHTROPE AND I ALWAYS REMEMBERED THAT. I JUST SAW IT AGAIN ON YOUR WEB SITE. CAN YOU EXPAND ON THAT?

You were always precocious and this is just another example, which I appreciate. Freud said there are only two instincts, the will to survive and the will to procreate.

That means that every human act follows into one or the other of those categories. That's what I meant.

When you write to me asking the answers to these questions, you might fall into either of those categories by that action or you might bridge the two, which is what most humans do in order to lead a less stressful life. We learn to contain our aggressive selves in order to have peace and rest from the struggle to survive, that is, the urge to procreation.

When my brother Al, who's in *Buffalo Nickel,* engaged in any activity at all, he sought the way to turn it to his advantage. That's an example of the will-to-survive personality. When Floyd in *Buffalo Nickel* decides to fight so he can keep his brother out of prison by having him be his trainer and engage in a wholesome activity with him, that is an act of the urge to procreation, because it's an act of love. That's what I mean.

EARLY IN YOUR CAREER, YOU CONTACTED A LOT OF PUBLISHED WRITERS AND OTHERS TO HELP YOU OUT. AFTER THE FIRST FEW SAID NO, WHY DIDN'T YOU GIVE UP?

First of all, I knew that I only meant good. I wasn't selfish. I wanted the best for the whole society. I wanted everyone to love each other like Jesus said. When some famous writers kicked me in the teeth, namely Ginsberg and Ferlingetti, when I asked for their help to publish my poems and they both turned me down, I scared Ginsberg. Ferlingetti was on a higher political plane in terms of real politics than I was—I mean in both poetry and the real world, a success at publishing and famous as a Beat

Generation guru. He—Ferlingetti—when I asked him to publish the poems, tried to tell me my early poems, which eventually got published, were psychopathic. And I knew he was a liar. And that he was looking for any way he could to reject me. So I knew then he was just part of the political machine—a "safe" radical—and that he did what he was told.

I had started the Student Peace Union at San Francisco State in 1962, and from that day on, I was hounded by the FBI. They never let up. They got to every source where I sought help in publishing my poems and my novel. But I knew that I was going to say something as great as Hemingway or Faulkner or D. H. Lawrence, whom I loved the most. And that what I wanted, I would find a place for it on the page and I would fulfill myself and not worry about rewards, whether they came or not.

When Ginsberg turned me down, too, because I scared him to death when I talked about cops, he made some critical comment that I don't even remember. That's how phony it was. And he said, "You scare me," on the phone before all that.

I knew that I was going to create or die. And nothing would stop me, not even death, because I meant no harm and my work would live on. I only meant good, for all, the living and those to come. Not just myself. That gives you great strength. And when it got tough and I wanted to kill myself and get it all over with, I had a belief in what I had to say—that it was important and it would create good in society. And I would be remembered for what I wrote. And I would get to give love and receive it.

CAN YOU DESCRIBE A FEW THINGS YOU'VE DONE OVER THE YEARS TO PROMOTE YOUR OWN WORK?

Not very much, probably. I'm not a businessman. I don't keep my mind on mundane things, like striving hard to get ahead. When you strive hard to get ahead, you lose sight of the forest for the trees and your work diminishes in quality because you are less than the person who wrote the first book. I wanted to spread love and spend my time doing what I loved before I died.

I try to make each day as eventful as possible, everything from running on a dirt path under the BART tracks to enjoying the birds that come into the trees in my yard. Or the squirrel who gets fat on my apples and eats every one off the tree. I still love him. And I like to keep myself in that state of contentment, in which I spend my time doing what I love. Because only love and time are priceless. That's the unstated oath that I try to live by: I try to spend my time doing what I love, which is love itself. This is all.

Actually, Claire says I have snatched defeat from the jaws of victory. After *Tattoo the Wicked Cross,* my first novel, came out, it was suggested, among other things, that I should apply for a Guggenheim, that I should teach at the Iowa Writers' Workshop, that I should apply for a tenure-track position at San Francisco State, etc. For one reason or another, I threw away every opportunity to get ahead because of my paranoid, non-cooperating rebel-writer stance, unlike some other famous writers, like the clown prince Ginsberg, who did what he was told.

WHAT DO YOU MEAN WHEN YOU CALL YOURSELF AN OUTCAST WRITER?

That means that everywhere I go, everyone I come in contact with will eventually, if not beforehand, cooperate in the suppression of my literature, one way or the other. And my radical unpublished novels that make *1984* and *Brave New World* seem real don't get published. But they are up on the Latino Web sites now, and why don't you check them out? I have two Spanish historical novels that could both be bestsellers and movies. But I don't have any confidence that it will happen unless I allow myself to be corrupted by sex and greed, the two tools that the secret police use to ensnare its victims, who no longer afterward have the purity of character they might have had before that degrading experience and no longer produce works of the same fine quality afterward. I try to avoid this by refusing to cooperate and so pay the price, and that is how my novels, like *Lay My Body on the Line* and *State of Emergency,* compare to *1984* and *Brave New World.* Check them out.

HOW DO YOU MAKE A LIVING?

That's a really personal question. I try to work as little as possible, and when I work, I try to work at what I love, which means teaching creative writing, fiction and poetry. That's essentially it, except that I bought some property with an NEA fellowship back in 1977 and I've been safe ever since. Once in a while, usually at the end of the year, I get some kind of royalty check or another. Like I said, this is very personal. Why should I tell you how I stay alive?

FLOYD'S ASSIGNMENT

write, read, edit, shape

Write spontaneously. That's the main key. Then read it. Then edit it. Then shape it into art. So the first thing you do is write it, first of all. Once you write it, it exists in its own "write," and I mean that as a pun, which also means "right." So there are five stages of this process of producing a work of art. The first is inspiration, energy, productivity. You write it down. You sit your butt someplace and you make it come out of your fingers some way, by pen or machine. That's the first advice I give. In order to write with the whole mind, the writer has to dare to face the truth behind his actions, whatever it was that made him or her what he or she is. He has to be honest, reporting what his mind tells him to write. He can't fake it in any way, meaning he can't slant it so he looks good. But this is also the time of the most intense subjectivity. Genius, in which the spontaneous spirit speaks without concern for any kind of censorship or compression.

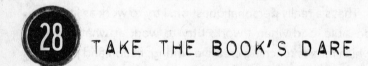

28 TAKE THE BOOK'S DARE

My books are the books that I am, the confused man, the negligent man, the reckless man, the lusty, obscene, boisterous, scrupulous, lying, diabolically truthful man that I am.

—**Henry Miller**

When I get an idea for a book or I'm working on a short story that has suddenly become unwieldy and I hear that distant wind-sound that tells me this is a book, I jump into the project with all the joy and fear of embarking on something brave. I could be quitting smoking, starting a new business, setting out to run a marathon. I'm a brand-new girl. I cannot fail. I write every day, write at every stoplight, write with the wind at my back. I come up with an outline, and then I write more.

That initial burst of energy usually takes me through the first fifty pages. And then I run out of steam. The fear begins to creep in. *Who will want to read this, anyway? What am I doing? This is self-indulgent and ridiculous. I don't even know where I'm going with it.*

Twice I have abandoned book projects at this point. I have the manuscript-starts in a file cabinet in my basement. Don't go and dig them up after I'm ashes in an urn. They're not worth the dead tree they're printed on. But seven other times I have continued.

I can feel the shadow of the exaltation I started the project with, but now I have to add discipline, too. I take comfort in something my teacher David Biespiel once told me: "You don't need to know where you're going with it."

I don't have to know where I'm going? A revelation! And so I carry on, with a dash of determination and equal parts hope and terror, and then I get to page 100. I'm not even numbering my pages at this point, but I've written enough books and counted back through enough pages to see the pattern: If I've got a huge mess on my desk and I'm convinced it's time to give up, this must be page 100.

Page 100 is not a good day.

These pages I have are by no means the first hundred pages of a book. They might be random pivotal scenes, mundane conversations, descriptions of cities my character has never seen. They are scraps. One hundred pages. The story I have and the story I have yet to tell are both too enormous for me to wrap my brain around. I curse David Biespiel's name. What the hell was he talking about, you don't need to know where you're going? Of course I have to know where I'm going! And so I put the project away for a week or a month, deflated. Once I abandoned a book project at this point. It's sitting there on my old orange Mac, waiting. But six other times I have continued.

I wake up one morning and I tell myself, "Ariel, you had a dream and it was a good dream. You wanted to write this book. You gave your spring and summer and autumn to the project, and I don't want you to quit now." I get up, print out my hundred pages. One hundred pages are a formidable thing to hold in your hands. I grab a pen, a pair of scissors, and a roll of Scotch tape before I head down to the corner bar and order an endless cup of coffee. I sit in the black vinyl booth and I read what I've got. I add a description here and a conversation there. I rearrange pages and paragraphs. I spread out scenes and chapters—take up a whole table. The bartender gives me a dirty look, so I order some tater tots as I begin to conceive of an outline. Sure, I had an outline going into the project, but that outline was tentative and unworkable. I need a serious outline now. I've given this book my heart and I'll be damned if I'm going to abandon my own heart over a little human confusion and frailty.

At home, I get back to my computer and input my new scenes. I rearrange. Sometimes I divide my document into parts or chapters. Little chunks of story I can actually wrap my mind around. I'm ready to do battle, to risk everything. I promise myself that all fates are possible at this point: This will be my masterwork, Random House will pay me the big bucks for it, or this will be my deliciously obscure treatise, I'll self-publish a thousand copies. Hell, maybe I'll hand-bind a single book for my friend China. It doesn't matter. What matters is that I set out to write a book and I'm going to write a book.

If I need some additional discipline, I join a writing workshop or convene a weekly writing group where I can bring in ten pages at a time. In doing so, I create a peer group of folks who are counting on my progress. In reality, they don't care if I show up empty-handed next week, but I set up a situation in which I have to prove myself. And I fall for my own trick.

My workdays become at turns exalting and painstaking, but I've hunkered down with this project and, as Marcy Sheiner says, "when I appear to be talking, I am often writing." I keep myself interested in the story by adding a turn or twist. I write scenes with obscure references. I throw in side stories I've always wanted to tell. I have fun. I remind myself how very much can go on in the space of a book. A two-page tangent isn't so much of a tangent. I screw around. I print out the whole manuscript and spend a day just making sure there's at least one weird metaphor on every page. I give my ex-boyfriend a blue beard so that any mythology buff who's paying attention will recognize him as Bluebeard from the original fairy-tale version of *Beauty and the Beast.* Of course, no mythology buff will ever be paying attention. I don't care. I'm spinning a tale for the perfect stranger in my imagination. Days when I don't want to write new scenes, I print out old ones and revise, rewrite. I switch the point of view from first person to third person and back again. And then. I run. Out of. Steam.

This is a pile of shit, this book. The perfect stranger doesn't exist. I've just wasted two years of my life. I hate my book and I hate myself even more. Other people can do this—*why not me?* Why didn't I go into some normal field of work? I could be a carpenter right now, a waitress, a lawyer. I have two options: suicide or . . . *what?* Okay. I'll continue.

If I've split up my pages into separate files, I know it's time to recompile it. Because . . . look! I have two hundred pages. Quitting now would be insane. So what if my book sucks? It's almost done! Now I'm writing like I'm sprinting. *I am sprinting.* I work late into the night and neglect my family. They wander in, offering eggplant and couscous for dinner, ask if I'm almost done.

"Almost," I promise. But I'm lying. Of course I'm lying. I don't know if I'm almost done. I could fail at any moment. The suspense keeps me up until I can't possibly hold my eyes open, and in the morning it pulls me out of bed and toward the bright hum of my computer. *Will I do it?* I can see something ahead—a light, a finish line, a *something.*

I'm on the verge of realizing my dream or I'm on the verge of going completely insane. There's no telling.

And then one night, a year or ten years after I began, the book is finished. Or at least I can't bear to look at it anymore. I go to bed and wake up sad because I've lost my good friend. Who will I tell my secrets to, now that my book is done? I revisit it, but it really is. Done. Or I'm done with it. Maybe I'll edit a little bit here and there. I'll rewrite. But our deep relationship is over. I'm as sad as a boiled egg. The book kind of sucks. It isn't the tour de force I first envisioned. It's a humble offering. But it's sweeter than I imagined, too. More human. It's the book that I am—the confused and messed-up book that I am instead of the goddess of a book I dreamed I could be. I grieve, but I'm psyched, too. My book is done! Oh my *God*. I wrote a book! It could be my first book or my sixth, and it's the same feeling: I fucking wrote a book!

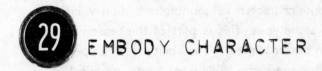

29 EMBODY CHARACTER

> It begins with a character, usually, and once he stands up on his feet and begins to move, all I can do is trot along behind him with a paper and pencil trying to keep up long enough to put down what he says and does.
>
> —**William Faulkner**

My new favorite book is *The Harmony Silk Factory* by Tash Aw, a masterful exploration of voice with a plot to keep you page-turning and a setting to open your soul. The truly bewitching thing about the book comes down to this: a character study of a textile merchant name Johnny Lim. Now, I don't care much one way or another about textiles or merchants, but it doesn't matter. Tash Aw knows this: In each person there is a hero and a villain. And it's the writer's job to explore the unique manifestation of that truth in the people we write about.

In the specifics—*does he read Whitman or play Pac Man?*—we find the general.

In the details—*is her manicure chipped or fresh?*—we see the whole.

In the depth-seeking dive into a unique soul we find, paradoxically, the universal stream that connects us all.

I mean, I *know* that textile merchant. And he's a total mystery to me.

Fantastic.

Our favorite characters in literature provide new insights into old archetypes. This is part of the reason writers often get better with age. The ability to "read people," which engenders the ability to "write people," is a learned skill, not an inborn talent. Life teaches us about character and the complexity of motivation. Experience shows us what we're capable of if we've got our back to the wall. Compassion is sometimes hard-earned.

If you want to learn to embody rich characters, listen to people. Observe them. Read ancient myths and modern novels. Question your own motivations. Guess at other people's agendas without judgment. Study the language of archetypes. But mostly live. And don't ever let the characters in your stories be any less weird than the folks in your life.

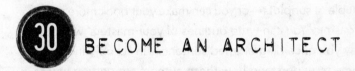

30 BECOME AN ARCHITECT

There are no rules in film making, only sins. And the cardinal sin is Dullness.

—**Frank Capra**

If you don't want to have to deal with character arc and plot, be a poet. That's it. Take your pick: plot or poet?

If you choose poet, you ought to read Miriam Sagan's book *Unbroken Line: Writing in the Lineage of Poetry.* Pretty soon you'll be churning out ballads and pantoums and villanelles and sestinas.

Oh, you mean you want to be a free-verse poet?

Forget it.

Even the freest of verse has a structure. Everything has a structure. The particular structure of prose—both fiction and nonfiction—usually comes down to character arc and plot. There's no getting around it. And why would you want to? Plot! Patterns from the scraps. Character arc: the change in the protagonist. Why tell your story if your character is the same man now as he was when you started? If nothing happens, who cares?

Now, short stories don't need complex plots. A subtle change or insight is enough to carry a short story. But a book needs some semblance of plot.

You can plot your book any way you like. You can focus on rising and falling action—a single central arc with a couple of subplots—or you can make your book more multi-orgasmic. You can write outlines of your masters' work the way you once diagrammed sentences in school, and you'll come to understand how these authors are getting you to turn each page. You can experiment with all kinds of structures. Even if you settle on a classical arrangement, you'll probably want to spice things up. Dramatic structure has gotten a bit stale since Aristotle's time—and staler still since screenwriters figured out how to use Joseph Campbell's *Hero's Journey* as a quick script formula—but it's still helpful to understand the traditional Western male story structure that so much of modern prose relies on. If you're miffed by the concept of plot or having trouble controlling your plot, the following cheat sheet might help. Dress it up with enough descriptive language, and no one will even notice you borrowed the bones. So here it is, demystified just for you, the classic five-act comedy:

Note that these "acts"—or parts of the story—don't have to be of equal lengths.

ACT I. CONTEXT

This is your background—or enough of the background so your reader won't get confused by the action. This act shows your character in her known world, in her daily life, in her culture or subculture. This is Dorothy in Kansas before the tornado. This is your first date when you're exchanging highlights of your life stories over Kung Pao vegetables.

ACT II. AWAY

Because background can be boring, Act Two can actually come before Act One—you can start out with "Away" and then backtrack to give us the context. In any case, this is your rising action. Your character faces a crisis and leaves something that is known for something that is unknown. She leaves home, is kidnapped, embarks on an adventure toward a goal, meets a new love interest, gets dumped by a current love interest, or experiences a trauma that will ultimately cause her to change and grow. This act shows your character diving or being pushed out of her element. This is Dorothy landing in Oz. This is the foreplay and we know we're going to get lucky.

ACT III. THE PLOT THICKENS

This act introduces a complication or further conflict. Here your character faces tests, bumps in the road, a temptation or distraction from the goal. This is the complication, but it may also be the heart of the story. If there are central lessons, they will be learned here. If there is a central battle, it will truly begin here. This is Dorothy crossing a fast-moving river, falling asleep in the poppy field, seeking an audience with the wizard. This act contains the moment when your new lover sees the jagged scar across your belly for the first time. This is the complication, but it also embodies the beginning of the climax.

ACT IV. DARKEST HOUR

Here's your worst-case scenario. In this act, it appears that the forces of "evil" will win out, the character will never reach her destination, the love will not survive, the character won't recover from the trauma. Total defeat. The wizard is a fraud. The new lover isn't coming! The new lover is having a heart attack!

Tragedies end here with dead lovers, lost heroes, the team of poor kids who've been practicing all year losing the big game, but we don't like tragedies. . . .

ACT V. DAWN COMES WHETHER WE WANT IT TO OR NOT

There is a turn of events—sudden or over time—that enables your character to resolve the problem, get to her destination or home again. Love survives, or the individual survives despite the failure of love. The character returns to his known world with some new knowledge—or he adjusts to life in the new world, and is free. He recovers emotionally from trauma, or has reason to hope. Classical stories often end with a wedding or a birth. But be careful with your resolutions—many a would-be great novel falls apart here. You don't need to tie up *all* the loose ends. And you don't need to get lazy and use a winning lottery ticket to get your character out of a jam. Let your character solve her own problems. Dorothy realizes she has what she needs within herself to get home. *Tap, tap, tap.* And you fall asleep in your lover's arms, satisfied.

31 GET CINEMATIC

Don't say the old lady screamed. Bring her on and let her scream.

—**Mark Twain**

Try thinking about your story as a movie. Where would it begin? Would the story proceed chronologically, as a series of flashbacks, or would it jump around through time? How many scenes would a screenwriter give to each event? A good screenwriter can condense decades into a couple of hours. How might she use a single dinner scene to suggest an entire family dynamic? Consider the voice-over. In movies, a voice-over comes in handy when the writer wants to *tell* us something rather than express it dramatically. There's nothing wrong with a pertinent voice-over—some screenwriters use them liberally, stylistically—but no movie is *just* a voice-over. I've read a lot of stories by beginning writers that are, essentially, just voice-overs. I close my eyes to listen, but still I can't see the particular red in their father's tie or the curl of their sister's lip. The writer will tell me it's 1983 when she might just as easily put leg warmers on the waitress, Ronald Reagan on the television, and "Do You Really Want to Hurt Me" blaring from the speakers of a passing Camero. It's fine if you want to tell me it's 1983, but why not *take me* to 1983?

When you see a movie you like, go and see it again. Pay attention to the way the screenwriter and the director and the actors give you the information you need. When somebody high on coke walks on set, nobody has to say, "This is John, he's high on coke." He's agitated. He's sniffling and wiping his nose. He looks like death, and from the jumpy swagger in his stride, we know he thinks he looks like George Clooney. If that's not enough, his sister might say, "John, are you on drugs again?" And John might say, "No way," *sniff sniff*. "You know I don't do drugs anymore." *Sniff sniff.*

Pay attention to the way a screenwriter tells the larger story, too. See if you can diagram the plot into three or five acts. Identify where we are being shown the character in his known world, at what point he is thrust into the world of the unknown, when the complication arises. Note the moment at which you, as the viewer, don't think she'll survive. And note how the writer manages to turn things around. Watch the movie a third time. Check your watch at each juncture. Are the acts of equal lengths? Screenwriters understand a lot more about plot and structure than most prose writers do. Start paying attention to their storytelling patterns.

32 THE TELL-ALL MEMOIR

An Interview with Michelle Tea

Michelle Tea is a master of conversational writing who moves between genres with a steady and engaging voice. Her signature style: high art cleverly disguised as gossipy dyke drama. Poetry, memoir, graphic novels, screenplays, zines, astrology columns, newspaper articles, fiction—Michelle pretty much does it all. The wildly prolific working-class author grew up in Chelsea, Massachusetts, ran away to zigzag the country, and landed in San Francisco in the early 1990s. There, amid the blossoming Mission District art scene, she had a revelation: She didn't have to go to college and have a book published by a big press to be a writer. She could be "this other kind of writer" who brings her work out into the streets, reads in bars, and publishes her own poetry. So that's just what she did.

In 1994 she and Sini Anderson founded the now-legendary poetry road show Sister Spit, a girls-only alternative to the boy-dominated spoken-word scene that dominated the city at the time. The slam-style extravaganza soon became the epicenter of creative expression for queer women writers and performers in the Bay Area. Meanwhile, Michelle's first book, *The Passionate Mistakes and Intricate Corruption of One Girl in America,* was being passed around college dorms and underground cafés, and heralded as the sweet and dirty vanguard of a new generation of subculture literature.

When her much-beloved autobiographical novel, *Valencia,* won a Lambda Literary Award for Best Lesbian Fiction and landed on the *Village Voice Literary Supplement*'s Top Twenty-five Books of 2000, Michelle had proven that "this other kind of writer" can be true to her working-class roots, loyal to the subculture art scene that taught her how to launch herself, and still find mainstream success.

I talked to her when she was on tour for *Valencia.*

WHAT INSPIRES YOU?

My own life, and the lives of the people around me. I'm starting to sniff out some more fictional ideas now, and I get lots of my inspiration from youth and poverty, basically, but even if I do start writing more fiction, I'm sure it will be fed heavily by events or people that are real. I'm just most inspired by reality, or maybe I have a weak imagination.

LAST TIME I SAW YOU, YOU WERE JOKING ABOUT STARTING A SAFE HOUSE FOR WRITERS, SOMEPLACE WHERE WE COULD ALL HIDE OUT AFTER WE'D WRITTEN OUR TELL-ALL MEMOIRS AND EVERYBODY HATED US. ARE YOU IN NEED OF A SAFE HOUSE THESE DAYS?

I have been feeling a little under siege since *Valencia* came out, but I think most of it is my own paranoia and insecurity about the book. Someone wrote anonymous mean little things about me on a flyer on my street, so for weeks I was feeling like, you know, the whole world hated my guts and I should never write again, but I am melodramatic and a baby also. I've gotten great feedback mostly, and I think there is only one ex-girlfriend portrayed in my book who wants me dead.

HOW DO YOU REMEMBER ALL THE DETAILS OF YOUR LIFE FOR A MEMOIR—DO YOU KEEP EXTENSIVE DIARIES?

I think I'm just lucky and blessed with a pretty good memory, because I can't keep a diary. I can't bear to—I've tried, and it's so painful to crack it open every day and see the carnage of yesterday's pathetic thought processes smeared across the page. It just really depresses me. I knew I wanted to be a writer when I was a little kid, and I remember reading an interview with Judy Blume in a kids' magazine and she was talking about how memory was so important to her writing and I held on to that.

HOW DO YOU OBSCURE THINGS?

I try not to obscure much, unless it is really going to be too revealing for people and hurt them, and even then it's still hard. For whatever reason, reality is what I am compelled to write about. I'm not very interested in making things up—my own imagination has never been much of a match for the reality of my life. To obscure things too much takes the fun out of writing for me. What I'm interested in is finding creative and compelling ways to talk about the truth.

HOW DO YOU PROTECT PEOPLE'S PRIVACY—DO THE CHARACTERS GENERALLY CONSENT TO BE INCLUDED IN THE STORY OR NO?

I do change people's names, and at times I have changed their hairdos and occupations, but if it is for some reason central to this person's character, or to my understanding of their character, it's hard for me to change it much because then it defeats the purpose. I can't remove the things that interested me in the person in the first place. And often the things that really drew me to a certain person, the things I want to write about, are very defining, and yes, it can reveal the person's identity despite the name change. I've removed things sometimes when I felt that including it would simply hurt the person and make them feel needlessly vulnerable without adding to the reader's understanding of who this person was to me. I don't really ask people if I can write about them or include them in a story. At this point people need to know what they're getting into when they hang out with me—I've been doing this for years! I did ask "Gwynn" if I could write about her cutting her arms, because that chapter was one of the first stories I wrote when I switched from poetry to longer pieces and I wasn't sure what was okay to write about and what was crossing a boundary. So I asked her and, being a writer herself, she of course just told me to write the truth, and that's what I try to do. My last girlfriend, who I just had a very messy breakup with, ordered me not to write about her. It'll be a while till I work up to that story anyway, and maybe she'll be more mellow about it by then.

HOW DO YOU CHOOSE YOUR STORIES?

I make a list of incidents, places, and people that seem like they would be interesting or important or fun to write about—[though] *fun* sounds like the wrong word. Just things that I feel like I could get very caught up and lost in writing about. I make a list of those compelling subjects and basically do "eeny meeny miny mo" and land on a story, and then I walk to the bar trying in my head to get back to the place I was at when I had that experience, and then, once in the bar, I read something short and inspiring and then I set down to writing till they kick me out.

MICHELLE'S ASSIGNMENT

secrets

In a workshop or writing group, have everybody write out a secret on a piece of paper. Mix them up and redistribute and have everyone write the story of the secret they got.

33 LATHER, RINSE, REPEAT

A first draft is written mostly for ourselves. We're jotting down the raw material, making a sketch, capturing the light or the basic outline of the subject. It's a kind of shorthand we set down so we won't forget the larger story we want to tell. Often we capture the initial energy we have for a project, and we have to be careful not to lose that in revision, but we also capture our own habitual linguistic quirks—the way we start every thought with "And then" or our addiction to the verb "to be."

Get out an old draft of something you'd like to work on again. Consider the arc of the story. What change occurs? Consider your opening. Do you have a warm-up paragraph there at the start you can nix now? If it's a short piece, cut it up into paragraphs and experiment with reordering scenes and events. Tape it back together. Check the beginning of each paragraph for repetitive language. Then read the whole thing and circle every use of the verb "to be." Rewrite the piece, getting rid of as many of the habitual starts, and as many instances of *was* and *is*, as you can. Sometimes you'll just be able to strip the *was* right out of the sentence. Sometimes you'll have to find another verb.

> *He was walking too quickly.*
>
> *He walked too quickly.*
>
> *I've never been more productive than I was in my early twenties.*
>
> *Productive years, my early twenties—I wrote for hours every night.*
>
> *I'm bored out of my mind.*
>
> *I stare off into space, bored out of my mind.*

Go through the piece again, this time looking for adverbs. Get rid of them.

> *He walked too quickly.*
>
> *He scampered ahead of me.*

Now read the piece out loud to yourself—read it monotone, not as if you're performing it. Are any of your sentences clunky? Where does the rhythm get lost? You can have some of your adverbs and your "to be" verbs back now, but this time you'll be adding them consciously.

As you're reading and rereading, you'll notice other things—a change of tone, a paragraph that needs to be moved, another one that needs to die, an anecdote that doesn't quite make your point, a chance to slow down and add dialogue and sensory details.

If you're working on a longer project—a book or a screenplay—you'll notice where you start to get bored. Even if you haven't worked on the piece for a couple of weeks, at certain junctures you'll want to skip ahead. Pay attention to that. If you're not interested in your work, it just might be humdrum.

If you're afraid of wrecking something, keep the original draft in a file. Keep a "cutting room" document on your computer where you can store your lost scenes. You probably won't ever need to retrieve them, but it's nice to know they're there.

Don't be embarrassed about the dorkiness of your draft. Don't take out the naked bits now, but don't be afraid to fix things and to experiment. You'd laugh if you saw my marked-up drafts, and you'd laugh even harder if you saw the reading copies of my published books. I never stop changing things. The most popular line in my performance version of my memoir, *Atlas of the Human Heart,* doesn't appear in the published book. I like to keep the work alive.

34 RELAX THE RULES

Forget grammar and think about potatoes.

—**Gertrude Stein**

Your elementary-school teacher loaded your book bag up with rules for writing (make sure you have an introduction, a body, and a conclusion). Your high-school English teacher stuffed in more (never start a sentence with *and* or *but*). And here I've added to your load. The reason for all these rules is simple: Human beings want to communicate with one another, leaving little room for misunderstanding. But rule-based grammar and punctuation can be such a drag.

I listen to my teenage writing students as they tumble into the classroom. They're chatting with friends in person and on cell phones, they're bopping their heads to the music on their iPods, they're text-messaging their mothers. They take their seats and I ask them to write me a poem. No problem. They can bring that pure and honest communication to the page. No one has ever told them that the rules of grammar extend to poetic forms. But the minute I say, "Tell me a story," half my students clam up. Prose means rules. And rules mean trouble. A sentence could actually be marked "wrong."

"Forget the rules," I say.

"Think about your story."

35 GET THE HELL BACK TO WRITING

An Interview with Dave Barry

The class clown of the American literary establishment, Dave Barry knows it's pretty funny that he won the Pulitzer Prize. But he *did*. I looked it up. And there it was on Pulitzer.org: "1988, Commentary, Dave Barry of *Miami Herald* for his consistently effective use of humor as a device for presenting fresh insights into serious concerns." How about that? He's also churned out twenty-five books and he plays lead guitar for the Rock Bottom Remainders, a literary band featuring Stephen King, Amy Tan, Ridley Pearson, and Mitch Albom. I've never heard them myself, but they claim to play music about as well as Metallica writes books.

DOES BEING A NEWSPAPER GUY—GETTING USED TO DELIVERING ON DEADLINE—HELP WHEN IT COMES TO WRITING IN OTHER MEDIA? OR DOES IT JUST GIVE YOU CHRONIC STRESS?

I think a newspaper background hurts you when you write books, because newspaper people tend to take deadlines seriously: If you're writing something for tomorrow's newspaper, you have to actually send it in before tomorrow. So when a book publisher tells you that your manuscript has to be done by, say, July 1, you think, *Wow! I had better get cracking on this!* But when you turn it in, the publisher sits around doing nothing with it for long periods of time, which is frustrating. So I have learned that, when I get a deadline from a book publisher, I should mentally add a certain amount of time, such as a decade.

I INTERVIEWED MARC ACITO, A.K.A. "THE GAY DAVE BARRY." ARE THERE A LOT OF OTHER DAVE BARRYS OUT THERE?

Hey! I thought I was the gay Dave Barry! But seriously, I think it's a wonderful thing, as long as all these people pay me the franchise fee.

HOW IMPORTANT IS CROSS-TRAINING IN OTHER CREATIVE FIELDS? IS PLAYING MUSIC JUST FOR FUN AND BLOWING OFF STEAM, OR DOES IT ACTUALLY HELP YOUR WRITING?

Playing music is good for my writing, because it reminds me that I am a really terrible musician and if I want to feed my family, I had better get the hell back to writing.

DAVE'S ASSIGNMENT

Floss.

36 ASK MAGNIFICENT METEOR

Rising Lit Star asks: Is writing talent nature or nurture? I keep thinking, *I am terrible*, but I don't practice. Sometimes I tell myself I would be a better writer if I had gone to get an M.F.A. Do you practice? If so, how? Does it make a big difference? Can you tell that you are becoming a better writer?

Magnificent Meteor reveals: There's a little bit of nature—the need and desire to tell stories—and then it's nurture all the way. You'd only be a better writer if you'd gotten an M.F.A. or journalism degree because you'd have been forced to practice. But you can make your own structure for practice. Blogging is practice. Writing letters is practice. Taking a writing workshop is practice. I have seen many so-so writers develop into fabulous storytellers in the space of a few ten-week workshops. Doing a zine is practice. Journaling isn't usually great practice, but it's better than nothing. Practice! But don't take my word for it—try it for twelve weeks and two issues of a zine and see for yourself.

Rising Lit Star asks: How do you find the time to dig deep enough to actually produce writing that's worth reading?

Magnificent Meteor reveals: Don't worry about "worth" while you're writing. I mean, sure, if you're bored, your reader will probably be bored, too, but if you're into the story you're telling, that energy will shine through. Digging deep doesn't have to be a time-consuming endeavor. The busier I get, the closer "deep" gets to the surface. I often write my favorite parts of a book in the middle of the night. It's helpful to have a night-light, and to sleep alone or have an amiable partner. Write when you're at the end of your rope—maybe you won't get a whole, cohesive story when you're having an emotional meltdown, but you might get the nugget that's going to make the rest of the story live.

Rising Lit Star asks: My struggle is sticking with a big project when there seems to be no light at the end of the tunnel. How do you stay motivated to finish a novel when there's no carrot on the end of your stick?

Magnificent Meteor reveals: When you sell a book on proposal, it's much easier to get through. You have a deadline! With literary nonfiction or a novel, you usually have to write the whole dang thing before you can sell it to a publisher or publish it yourself. For me it's sometimes helpful to simply *know* I will publish. Because of the economics—or, rather, because of *my* economics—I prefer to find an outside publisher for my books, but I promise myself that if I can't interest an established press in the final product, I'll put it out myself. This frees me up from worrying about mainstream acceptability while I'm working, and it seems to satisfy the part of my ego that screams, "You're wasting your life! This book will languish in your desk for eternity!" Other times I get to wondering if *any* kind of publication would be a good idea for such a tangled mess of words. When I get to that place, I sign up for a writing workshop or convene a weekly writing group. I may not be looking for all that much feedback on the work, but with the group I can create a situation where I have to bring in, say, a chapter a week. It gives me a regular deadline and a small audience for those crucial few months when I'm in danger of abandoning a pretty good idea.

Rising Lit Star asks: How do I know if it's good? And how will I know when to quit if it isn't?

Magnificent Meteor reveals: You won't know. Creativity is high-risk. And "good" is subjective. A background in punk philosophy helps here: You don't have to be good at something to do it. Put your heart into your work, don't take yourself too seriously, and practice.

PART THREE

publish before you're ready

We have to continually be jumping off cliffs and developing our wings on the way down.

—Kurt Vonnegut

37 MAKE A FOOL OF YOURSELF

I like publishing because it is possible to survive one's mistakes.

—Michael Joseph

If I stayed home with the curtains drawn until I'd written, rewritten, and polished to perfection each precious line of the next Great American Novel, I wouldn't be famous enough to get it published. As it is, when I do produce my finest masterpiece, folks will say, "I always knew Ariel Gore had it in her," and the *New York Times* will admit that I'm a genius, and I'll be even more famous than I had to be to get the thing published, and I can die a goddess.

Until then, I'll publish what I've got.

Most lit stars' first publications were straight-up embarrassing. This is as it should be. You live and learn. The humiliation of a bad poem doesn't truly hit home until your ex-husband has submitted it in family court as evidence of your total mental incapacity.

I will not write such a poem again.

But even the embarrassment is good practice. If you're going to be famous, you'd better get used to humiliation. There is no dignity in celebrity. When I finally got the *L.A. Times*—my grandmother's hometown newspaper—to run a big color picture and proclaim me a lit star, they also mentioned that I'd once slept with a man for money. *Thank you.*

"The unread story is not a story," Ursula K. Le Guin says. "It's little black marks on wood pulp." So make your little black marks live. Let a reader turn them into a story.

Look around. Great people are always kicking themselves for failing to reach impossible standards of perfection while the mediocre ones run around doing this and that and seem never to feel the least bit bad about themselves.

So your first published piece won't be in *The New Yorker.* So what? Maybe it will be in a small community newspaper published out of someone's dirty kitchen, and the only way you'll get them to print it is by volunteering to do the dishes. It might be in a niche magazine or a small-circulation national zine called *I (heart) Amy Carter,* it might be in a self-published chapbook. It doesn't matter. Get used to publication. Get used to writing for strangers. Get used to the stupid things those strangers will tell you about your work. Get used to the awesomely heartening things they'll tell you. Get used to the fact that as a writer, you may never know who read your work and whether or not it had any impact on them at all. Get used to imperfection. Get used to the typos that make it past copy editors. Get used to publication. Short stories.

Articles. Blogs. Columns. Blurbs. Poems. Whatever you've got. If you want to write for strangers, get it out there so those strangers can see it.

A lot of glossy magazines won't even read your stuff if you don't have a résumé. But here's the good news: You can publish the first issue of your zine for fifty dollars. If you've got access to the Internet, you can start a blog for free. Once you're publishing stuff yourself, you're not just a writer, you're a writer-publisher. If you publish other people's stuff, too, you're a writer-editor-publisher. You can join the club. And a listserv. You can go to potlucks with other writer-editor-publishers. You can offer to review books and write fillers for *their* zines and journals and Web sites. And voilà! You've got a résumé.

When it comes to writing a book, just write it. If the book is nonfiction, you might be able to write a proposal for it and get a contract before you write the whole thing. More likely, if it's your first book, you'll just have to write it. And what about when it's done? Try to get an agent. An agent can try to sell the book to a big press and get you a little money. And what if you can't get an agent or don't want one? So what? I know a few people who've spent years-coming-on-decades trying to find an agent who'll sell their book to a huge press. They won't even consider going for a medium or small press. This is madness. I don't understand it. Maybe they're hoping to impress their parents. But I can tell you that if your parents are not proud of you as an unpublished writer, they will not be proud of you as a published writer. If they are picky, critical people, they will find fault with your book regardless.

Maybe these developing writers want to make a lot of money. If so, they ought to learn a trade. Big presses are great, but they're not the only game in town. Start with a humble book at a humble press. Start with your own press. Make three hundred copies. Call a local bookstore and set up an author event. Invite all your friends. Make flyers to advertise it. Send press releases and review copies to relevant media. Sell your three hundred copies. And use the money to print more. Now you're a published author. *Onward!*

Your first published pieces will be incomplete and imperfect. Who cares? It's better to make a fool of yourself in front of a small audience than it is to steal from the world the light of your coming brilliance.

38 WRITE FOR STRANGERS

Like most writers, I started out writing for myself. I kept messy, irregular, emotional diaries. I meditated, pen in hand, across pages lined and blank. I free-associated and rambled on. But eventually, journaling to become a writer started to feel like playing with buckets of salt water to become a surfer. Sure, I had to get used to the elements I wanted to work with, but freewriting can only take a writer so far. So I started penning letters to friends, writing poems and posting them on telephone poles, and then, finally, writing short articles and profiles for *Sonoma*

County Women's Voices, a small community newspaper where the editors were kind enough to give me an internship.

Occasionally when I'm stuck on a story or a chapter now, I'll open a notebook and scrawl stream of consciousness to empty my mind and let the universe fill the vacuum, but it's usually more helpful to take a walk, have sex, paint a portrait, lift weights, go out for a drink. Freewriting helped me recover from too many years of formal education, but it's no longer a super-effective tool when it comes to waking my creative brain.

If you want to write just for yourself, that's fine. Get a good journal. Archival quality. But if you want to write for strangers, too, you'll have to publish. I've had teachers who warned writers not to publish until they're "ready." This is silly. What's "ready"? I started publishing my work long before I was ready. Start publishing. Start right away. And don't be afraid to start small. Set yourself up with a public diary at livejournal.com. Print poetry on stickers and post them around town and in bathrooms. Print short-short stories on well-designed bookmarks and convince local booksellers to display the freebies on their counters. Print your words on anything you can think of—paper, walls, or the pages of cyberspace—and distribute freely.

39 START SMALL

As Marc Acito says, it's not who you know in this business, it's who knows you—or rather, who knows your writing. So don't be afraid to start small.

I might need a famous author to blurb a new book. I might find that author's Web site and send him an e-mail introducing myself and asking if he wouldn't mind taking a look at my manuscript and consider endorsing it. And that famous author might write back saying, "Sure, I know you. You wrote that weird short story in *Fly by Night* magazine six years ago. . . ." This is exactly three trillion times better than trying to get that same famous author to remember that we shook hands once. No agent, editor, publisher, or writer has ever said to me, "Sure, I know you. We met at such and such literati cocktail party. . . ."

Even if no one who'll be specifically helpful to you ever reads your weird short story in *Fly by Night* or your column in the PTA newsletter, you're taking your craft and your genius into the world now. You're getting used to seeing your words in print. If you have an editor, you are learning how to be edited—how to revise when asked, how to let the little changes go, how to fight for your original words when they're truly important to you. When you read your first articles in print, you may notice that they seem to have a different rhythm and tone to them now that they're set in type. A story on a magazine page has a different feel to it than a story on the computer screen. That's because written words and stories are living things. You can't always control the editing or the subtle transmutation that takes place when a piece is printed, but you can get used to the process and begin to work with it. If my first published work had been a book I'd spent years working on, I probably would have had a nervous breakdown. As it was, my first published article happened to be a six-hundred-word story about a local First Nation farm struggling for survival. It took me a week to write. The subject matter was important to me but not deeply personal. And so I began to learn to publish and be published not with a huge splash but with a small offering, by lending my still-shy voice to an unseen community treasure that needed every voice it could get.

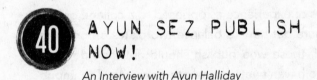

40 AYUN SEZ PUBLISH NOW!

An Interview with Ayun Halliday

Probably best known as the mama behind the *East Village Inky,* the handwritten and -illustrated zine about family life in New York, Ayun Halliday started her creative career as a theater geek. Back in Chicago, she was a member of the Neo-Futurists, a company notable for presenting thirty original plays in sixty minutes and ordering pizza for the audience whenever the show sold out. But the Midwestern native had New York City dreams, and in the early nineties, she and fellow Neo-Futurist Greg Kotis got married, moved into a 340-square-foot studio apartment in Greenwich Village, and promptly started making babies.

On daughter Inky's first birthday, Ayun put out the first issue of her zine, and she's been publishing ever since. I just got issue #30 in my post-office box today! Her books include a book of mothering tales, *The Big Rumpus,* a book of traveling tales, *No Touch Monkey!,* and *Job Hopper: The Checkered Career as a Down-Market Dilettante.*

HOW IMPORTANT IS PUBLICATION TO YOU?

Very! Because I need people to read what I've written. I write a lot in journals, but that's to preserve my life (it's amazing how quickly I forget it), with the side effect that it keeps me toned up as a writer. If you don't publish, you will never earn any money as a writer. Also, it seems to me true that if you publish, you are a "real" writer, a waitress with years of experience as opposed to a college girl trying to figure out how to balance two plates on one arm. That said, those who publish should not look down on those who haven't yet—for whatever reason. The unpublished may still call themselves writers and hold their heads high!

DO YOU RECOMMEND SELF-PUBLISHING?

Yes! Because, to paraphrase Spalding Gray, I got sick of waiting for the big infernal machine to make up its mind about me. I just wrote sixteen or so pages on this topic, and it's a big, sprawling mess. I believe in the DIY ethic, and it certainly leads to a more gratifying quality of reader feedback, often on very unusual stationery.

WHAT ADVICE/WARNINGS WOULD YOU HAVE FOR A YOUNG WRITER JUST STARTING OUT?

Start your own zine and work to promote it. Read a lot. Keep a journal. Maybe try to get a job working at a magazine or publishing company. I think connections can't hurt, although maybe this is the POV of a longtime waitress with a bachelor's in theater.

Warnings? Don't take too many older or more experienced people's warnings to heart, because it's very likely their advice is the viper of ego, disguised. Don't succumb to your own inherent laziness. In my personal opinion, the best writers never forget that life is at all times complex.

AYUN'S ASSIGNMENT

fun and free

1. Choose something you're sure to see lots of in your neighborhood or someone else's neighborhood and go there, armed with a notebook, a digital camera, a sketch pad, whatever will help cement the impressions of the things you saw on your "safari." Early issues of the *East Village Inky* documented my findings from a self-assigned T-shirt safari in the souvenir/head shops of St. Mark's Place and a survey of everything you could get for a quarter from the gumball machines of First Avenue. Fun! Free!

2. Go home and record your impressions on both sides of a single sheet of paper, leaving at least a quarter-inch margin all the way around. Eschew the computer in favor of a black felt-tipped pen. Now you don't even have to go home! You can fulfill this portion of the assignment in a café, on a park bench, at school or at work. I don't recommend trying to do it on the bus or subway, but only because the forward motion will joggle your hand, so everyone who sees the resulting penmanship will assume that you were drunk. Free yourself from the convention of how something like this should look. Illustrate it as poorly or as well as you are able, draw arrows, add parenthetical asides as they occur, and allow your "font size" to dwindle if that's what it takes to squeeze in everything you want to say.

3. Xerox at least twenty copies. Mail at least five to friends, acquaintances, and/or reviewers. Leave a complimentary stack where interested parties might happen upon them. Congratulations. You are now self-published. The big, infernal machine has nothing on you!

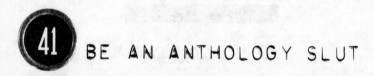

41 BE AN ANTHOLOGY SLUT

Submit your short stories and essays to anthologies. When you get a piece in an anthology, you get a publishing credit, a "real book" your friends can buy at Powells.com, and sometimes you even get fifty bucks. It may seem counterintuitive, but often the competition to get your work into an anthology is actually *less* fierce than it is to get it into an established magazine or journal. This is because the calls for submissions for anthologies go out and stay out for just a few months. The procrastinators are out of the game from the get-go. When you submit to *Zyzzva,* you're up against the hermits who've been working on their three-paragraph story for ten years.

Beyond actually submitting—rather than thinking you'd like to submit—there's plenty you can do to up your odds of acceptance. First, you've got to understand a little bit about what it's like to edit one of these collections. An anthology editor has a vision, right, a topic he wants to do a book about, but he doesn't want to write the whole thing himself. He wants a diverse but thematically coherent group of stories on said topic. He wants a good book that's fun to read. So he pastes flyers up around town and in creative writing departments, maybe puts an ad in a writers' magazine or posts the news of the upcoming anthology online. Maybe he's got an agreement from a publisher for publication and maybe he doesn't. It's better for us if he does, of course. You can waste a lot of time writing stories for anthologies that will never see the light of print. But that's life.

The good news is that most anthology editors, unlike many magazine editors, actually read most of the submissions they get. Since they're not full-time editors, they're still excited about the process and haven't yet gotten buried in stories they can't use and jaded by the few psycho junk-mailers who write incoherently off-topic and submit and submit and submit. To benefit from these editors' excitement, it's best to send your submission a week or two before the deadline. On Deadline Day, they're going to be swamped. A week or two beforehand, they're still leisurely drinking their morning coffee, waiting for a new voice to lift them right out of their chairs.

Start by doing a quick online search for anthology submission calls, check Web sites of anthology publishers you like, and look for ads in publications like *Poets & Writers.* You'll find plenty of things you're not qualified to write—an anthology of essays by women in mechanics does you no good if you're a man in hairdressing—but I go for topics that I can "sort of" fit into as well as those that sound like they were conceived of just for me. Here's a sampling of anthology themes I found today:

- "Looking for essays and stories by parents of children with autism"
- "Seeking poetry, short stories, and anecdotes by Black and Asian writers from the North of England on the subject of hair"
- "Submit your true angel stories!"
- "Looking for stories and perspectives on teen parenting"
- "New anthology seeks '20-something' stories about how you see life in between college and 'settling down'"
- "Calling all hitch-hikers, train-hoppers, runaways, wanderers and adventurers. I'm looking to compile personal accounts of low-budget and long-term travelers."

All right. I've got an angel story I could polish and a hitchhiking adventure I could whip up. No problem.

Read the call for submissions carefully before you get to work. Your story must fit into the editor's vision of the project. Often a call for submissions will list what the editor *isn't* looking for. The hitchhiking anthology will not include stories about study abroad, "the time my parents paid for me to go to Europe," or anything high-budget. You want your story to fit into the parameters of the editor's call, but you also want it to stand out. Maybe you've got an angle the editor hasn't even thought of. Emphasize your difference. If I hitchhiked with a baby or hopped a train to get to my mother's funeral, that's going to get me more "unique" points than the standard college dropout who gets inspired by Kerouac.

If you want to write a piece about your experience as a train-hopper and you've done it a hundred times, you'll want to tell one specific tale that reads like good fiction. "The time I hopped a train to Chicago and wound up in a jail in Tijuana" might be right up this editor's alley.

In the call for submissions, you'll also likely find a word limit. My strategy for anthology submissions is to submit something well under the word limit. If the editors say they'll consider up to three thousand words, I shoot for fifteen hundred to two thousand. If they say they want stories between two thousand and five thousand words, I go for two thousand, sometimes a little less. I don't want my piece to be so short as to throw off the balance of the book, but I know that a fifteen-hundred-word story in the "maybe" pile has a much better chance of getting into the "yes" pile. As an unknown writer, you're asking the editor to take a risk on your work, after all, and if you're only asking for five pages—well, that's a manageable risk. *How about this little one by the train-hopper in a wheelchair,* the editor might think. *A little rough around the edges, but it's unique, it tells a story, and, hey, what's fifteen hundred words?*

Not every story you write for an anthology is going to get accepted, so don't waste time writing about your Asian hair in the North of England if the subject doesn't inspire you. But writing for anthologies is a great way to get over the whole "What am I going to write about?" whine and an even better way to start getting your work out into the world.

42 MAKE A ZINE

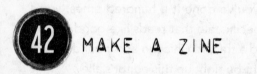

Freedom of the press is guaranteed only to those who own one.

—A. J. Liebling

As a young writer, the business was explained to me thusly: You spend weeks and months and sometimes years writing and polishing the story closest to your soul and then you stick it in a manila envelope—sure to include a SASE and a pithy cover letter—and you send it out to a stranger at a highbrow literary journal. At home, you pace and pray, hoping for a miracle. "That's just the way it's done," folks told me. But does a fledgling visual artist just send out slides and queries to famous galleries and the Museum of Modern Art? No! He goes down to his local café and hangs the work himself. Better yet, he opens his garage or studio apartment and invites a bunch of friends over for his first big show. Why, then, are young writers encouraged to rely on strangers to get their first rants into print? I'll tell you why: dumb tradition. It's a custom that originated back in the days when not everyone knew someone who knew someone who owned a printing press. A hundred years ago, you could live, write, and die anonymously without ever gaining access to the means of publication. In an age of computers at the library and photocopiers at 7-Eleven, you have no such excuse.

I have nothing against manila envelopes and highbrow literary journals. By all means, send your stories out to friends and strangers! Go down to your local independent bookstore and look at all the magazines. Find the ones you like and read them. Check the masthead for the submissions editor and write a cover letter explaining what you love about the publication and why readers would delight to find your words in its pages. But you can start your own highbrow publishing house, too. You don't need an office. You don't even need a computer of your own. I was a single mom on welfare when I made the first issue of *Hip Mama*. My daughter was eleven when she created her first successful zine—*Love and Death in Fifth Grade*. Making a zine is fun. It's rewarding. It's a lot of hard work for very little pay. So let's roll up our sleeves and get started!

WHAT'S A ZINE?

It's an independent publication (pronounced zeen!) that can contain stories, articles, poems, artwork, photos, collages, stickers, and anything else your heart desires.

A zine can be a magazine, a newsletter, a broadsheet, a book, or a portfolio.

The first step in making your zine is familiarizing yourself with the genre. Independent bookstores in most American cities carry an array of these small, noncommercial publications. In Portland, Oregon, the Independent Publishing Resource Center houses the largest zine library in North America. At nearby Reading Frenzy, you'll find hundreds for sale. In Baltimore, Atomic Books is Zine Central. And in Chicago, Quimby's is your source. If there's no zine shop in your hometown of Buttonwillow, visit any of these shops online, by going to their individual Web sites or to microcosmpublishing.com. Peruse the titles and see what appeals, or order a few of my favorite zines:

Farm Pulp—Some of the best creative writing in a zine today—and always in an intriguing format.

Send three dollars to Gregory Hischak.
Farm Pulp
P.O. Box 2151
Seattle, WA 98111-2151

Invincible Summer—Nicole Georges's gorgeous art and handwritten adventures.

Send five dollars to Nicole J. Georges.
P.O. Box 12763
Portland, OR 97212

Rad Dad—Tomas's reflections on radical fatherhood.

Send two dollars to Tom Moniz.
1636 Fairview St.
Berkeley, CA 94703

Tenacious—Writings from women in prison.

Send two dollars to V. Law.
P.O. Box 20388
Tompkins Square Station
New York, NY 10009

Xtra Tuf—The zine for commercial fishing women!

Send five dollars for the whopping 192-page issue
#5 to Microcosm Publishing.
P.O. Box 14332
Portland, OR 97293

CONTENT

Once you've dipped your toes into the zine world with a few issues of *Deep South Mouth* or *The Future Generation,* it's time to decide what kind of zine *you* will make. You can choose a theme and accept submissions, or write everything yourself. Some writers publish chapters of their novels-in-progress as zines, while others use the medium as a kind of public journal. You won't need too much material for your first issue—you want to keep your printing costs low—so you might want to select one or two short stories or a dozen poems you've written. Don't feel compelled to include other writers in your zine—some of the most delicious zines out there are penned by a single author—but if collaboration inspires you, invite a couple of friends to contribute their own short pieces. In addition to the main dishes—the stories closest to your soul—you'll want to include appetizers, like a table of contents and an introductory "hello" thanking your reader for picking up your new publication. You'll want side dishes, too, visual elements to keep the reader interested, and shorter pieces of writing like news items, quotes, quizzes, and reviews. Zine publishers know that the final page of a publication—not the first page—is the most widely read. Plenty of readers skip the green beans, but no one skips the pecan pie! They flip to the back while they're still in line waiting to buy the thing, so your last page should be self-contained, not just a continuation of a longer story. Big magazines often use the back page for their humor column. You can do what you like, but remember: The last course of your zine should be yummy.

FORMAT AND LAYOUT

Your zine can be any color, shape, or dimension. Your printing process can be mimeograph, photocopy, silkscreen, or offset. Your text can be handwritten, typed, or laid out on a computer. Your zine should be big enough to read but small enough to carry. A common-size zine is 5½ by 8½ inches, referred to in the printing business as "half standard" because it's standard 8½-by-11-inch sheets folded in two. Or you can choose a "standard" size—11-by-17-inch sheets folded. You should know that the reason newspapers and magazines usually lay out their text in columns is that the human eye tires if it has to follow a horizontal line across a page for more than about four inches. So if you use a standard-size format, consider breaking your text up into two columns. Other tricks to keep readers from getting overwhelmed with text are to include a visual element—a photo or a drawing—on most pages, to use ten- to thirteen-point type for your body text, and not to be afraid to leave white space here and there. Look at zines and magazines you enjoy reading and copy their design. Count the number of words the publishers put on each page and don't try to cram many more onto your own pages.

PRODUCTION

For a short-run publication—anything under five hundred copies—photocopying is going to be your most cost-effective printing choice, but your zine can still look tough. To make your low-budget publication stand out, use colored paper for the cover or include a color-Xeroxed inset. If you don't have free access to a copy machine, call around to various shops in your town to see who can do it inexpensively. The cheapest copy shop in my town charges just under four cents a copy, and another four cents for color paper, so if I make a twenty-four-page half-standard-size zine with a color cover, printing will run me forty-eight cents per zine. With a hundred copies for a first pressrun, I'm out about fifty bucks, but now I'm a published author! I'm an editor/publisher! I rule!

DISTRIBUTION

The first and easiest way to distribute your new zine is to give it to your friends and family. Only give them one copy each, and then include ordering information in the back in case they want more. Yep, Great-Grandma's first copy is free, but if she wants to pass it around at the old folks' home, it's two dollars a pop. If you don't mind passing out a few more free copies, ask the managers at your local record stores or cafés if you can leave a stack. Getting rid of a free zine isn't hard to do, but if you want to get paid for your efforts—or at least get a fraction of your investment back—you're going to have to figure out how to sell this puppy for cash. A cover price (printed on the cover!) and ordering information prominently displayed in the back is imperative. Once you've got those basics in place, paid distribution is going to happen in four ways: consignment, mail order, third-party distribution services, and hand sales. Consignment means that you get paid when and if the zines sell. Take your zine to all of your local bookstores and ask them to sell it on consignment. Some of them will say no. Don't trip. Others might say yes. Keep track of how many zines you've left at each bookstore and come back once a month to collect your dollars and bring more zines if they need them. Mail-order sales are easier to deal with. Someone sends you money and you send them a zine. Some folks will order your zine in the mail simply because they've found a free copy and want another; others will find your address online or on a zine-review zine (you can find currently publishing zine-review resources by searching online; as I write this, *Factsheet 5*, the legendary guide to the zine revolution from the eighties and nineties, had plans to resume publication). If you have a particularly snazzy or simply excellent zine that bookstores beyond your local area can sell, you'll be able to find a national distributor to do the sales and delivery legwork for you. I hesitate to give you a list of national zine distributors here, because they tend to go out of business. Do an Internet search for current distribution services, but do remember that these outfits can be short-lived. Never send a distributor more copies of your zine than you can afford to lose. Distributor copies are almost always *distributed*—getting you exposure and mail-order sales—but oftentimes you'll never actually see a check for the copies sold. This is true for both large and small distributors. I've been in this business a long time, and I've seen many, many zines and magazines rise and fall to their deaths because they broke the cardinal rule: They sent more copies than they could afford to lose to *Fine Print* or *Desert Moon* or *Big Tent*—all great distributors that died tragic deaths and took more than a few small publishers down with them. This brings us to the fourth and most excellent mode of paid distribution: good, old-fashioned hand sales. Someone gives you two crumpled dollars and you hand them a zine. Every publisher's favorite way to do business. But where will you meet these readers and customers? you ask. You'll meet them at your . . .

ZINE RELEASE PARTY!

You can have your zine release party at home, but who wants to vacuum for guests? Better to go down to your local café, bar, winery, restaurant, or bead shop and ask them to host your party for you. They'll sell a few extra cups of coffee or beer—or a few extra beads—and you'll have the benefit of a public venue in which to launch your zine. Invite all your contributors, family, and friends. Invite strangers, too. Send out announcements to local writers, teachers, and publishers. Get your event listed in your local papers. Post flyers up and down the street. Offer good music and free apples or something. Put on a show! Read from your new zine and get everyone to buy it. This is your debut, your coming-out party, your launch! If no one shows up, try it again somewhere else. Hand sales is where it's at. And a party makes it all worthwhile.

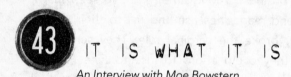

43 IT IS WHAT IT IS

An Interview with Moe Bowstern

When I moved to Portland, Oregon, it seemed as if the first question on everybody's lips was: "Have you met Moe yet?"

"No," I had to admit. "Who's Moe?"

"A pirate."

"Storyteller."

"A singer."

"Organizer of the Amalgamated Everlasting Union Chorus."

"Fisher poet."

"Puppeteer."

"She was in that indie movie, riding her bicycle naked—remember?"

"She makes that zine *Xtra Tuf*."

Oh, yeah. I know that zine! But I wouldn't meet its maker for a while yet—she wasn't in town.

If you don't live in Portland, Chicago, Pittsburgh, or Kodiak, you might not know Moe Bowstern—but you should. A local lit star with anarchist anti-fame tendencies, she's been chronicling the inside story about being a commercial fisherwoman and spinning traveling tales for years. If you ever need to know the proper way to remove a whale from your salmon net, Moe's your woman. And if you ever have any questions about putting out a zine, just drop her an old-fashioned letter in the snail mail. When she gets back in town, she's bound to answer you.

I HEARD THAT YOU HAD VOWED NOT TO START A ZINE. WHY WAS THAT? AND WHAT MADE YOU CHANGE YOUR MIND?

When I first encountered zines in the late eighties, it seemed to me that editors were always asking for submissions. Here, I thought, was a great place for me to practice writing. I'd submit pieces to various zines. Sometimes I wrote some story down that I liked to tell, sometimes I wrote a story that reflected the theme of the zine. I felt like there were plenty of zines in the world that needed writers, and the world was better served by more good writing in existing zines than by yet another zine.

In 1995 I hooked a friend of mine up with a deck job on the salmon boat where I was the skiff operator. My friend was an artist who drew almost compulsively. Doodles and fantastic sketches, all fish-related, sprouted constantly from her pen. We shared a house at the time with a scholar/deckhand and an artist who had traveled up from

Chicago with me. Our little shack, affectionately named the Leaky Hovel (we had five five-gallon buckets catching leaks in a two-room shack), was full of art and music. I had arrived that spring to fish herring and would stay through the end of September salmon fishing. Creating a zine was an idea that I felt would help me pace myself through six months of fishing, give a theme and a structure to the summer. My friends thought it was fun, and we operated in zine-planning mode throughout the season. It was helpful to be among artists for almost the entire time I was in Kodiak, from late March until the first week of October. In the years since I read my first zine, I began to realize also that one could create a literary landscape within one's own zine and there declare one's true self. I think I was finally ready to do that. After years of shuttling between my winter life as an artist and my summer life as a deckhand, I could, in creating a zine with my peers, declare myself an artist in raingear, a deckhand who dealt in words, pictures, and music as well as fish.

HOW HAS DOING *XTRA TUF* HELPED YOU AS A WRITER? HAS IT HELPED YOU HONE YOUR STYLE OR GET EXPOSURE YOU MIGHT NOT HAVE GOTTEN?

One of the biggest ways I feel that *Xtra Tuf* specifically and writing about fishing in general has challenged me is in trying to decode the jargon and lifestyle of a commercial fishing boat so that nonfishing people can understand my stories and fishing people can still hear their own experiences reflected back at them without getting bored. I've also learned to write long narratives that describe daily life, rather than punchy short stories complete unto themselves. In *Xtra Tufs* #3 and #5 I've condensed existing recorded and experienced histories into narrative form to set backgrounds for subsequent parts of the zine.

The zine has opened many doors for me. It put me in touch with the Fisher Poets Gathering, an annual literary performance event that takes place each February in Astoria, Oregon. Being part of that event led to my inclusion in the Northwest Folklife Foundation's annual Folklife Festival in Seattle when they featured participants in maritime cultures from Maine to Savoona Island in the Bering Sea. Zine stories I've written have been accepted into anthologies and published in the *Alaska Fisherman's Journal. Xtra Tuf* has also gone before me in the underground literary world and the national and international zine scene. People everywhere know and love *Xtra Tuf,* which probably gets me a place to stay in lots of towns.

CAN YOU GIVE US SOME IDEAS FOR ZINE DISTRIBUTION?

Well, I feel like there are a lot of people with more efficient distribution plans. For years I just passed my zines out wherever I went. I finished the first two issues right before I went fishing, so sprinkled them across the country from Chicago to Kodiak. I traded them for coffee at cafés, I left them in bathrooms at houses where I was a guest or at restaurants where my friends worked, I took them to independent bookstores or left piles with friends. I send them to other zine editors whose work I admire. I send them on tour with my friends' bands, or I give them to friends on road trips to help them pay for their travel. After a while I began to get requests from small distributors for five or ten zines here and there. A year or so ago, Microcosm Publishing started to carry *Xtra Tuf* and my two other zines, *This Little Light of Mine* and *Second Set Out.* They are very thorough in their coverage of independent bookstores and infoshops across the United States and in the United Kingdom. This frees me up to work on more art projects and, frankly, I sag on the administrative end of *Xtra Tuf.* It's unfortunately commonplace for me to find a two-year-old letter in some box of mail in my office with a polite and earnest request for a zine. I send a dozen apologies in a year and always try to follow through—even if it takes a few letters. Usually the amount at risk—what people send me—is less than five dollars, but it's more about trying to keep the promise of zine culture. If you write me a letter, I will write you a letter and send a zine. Nowadays I ask people to get zines from Microcosm, but still invite them to write to me.

Rebecca Gilbert (creator of *Verboslammed* zine, *Napcore* zine, and printer at Stumptown Printers) told me the best idea I ever heard about for zine distribution. It was for a gas jockey zine. In Oregon, drivers don't pump their gas, they wait for an attendant, or gas jockey. Rebecca told me about an attendant who stuck tiny little zines about being a gas jockey inside the little door on the car that protects the gas cap. Thus it was passed as a parasite to the next gas jockey at the next fuel pump, with the driver none the wiser.

I've also known people to make comics or zines that look like bus schedules, which are then slipped into racks among genuine bus schedules. I think Aaron Cometbus used to create a library catalog card for his zine so he could sneak it into library systems that required ISBN numbers. Obviously, computer systems render that last method obsolete, but it might work in some small, stubborn library somewhere.

ISSUE #5 OF *XTRA TUF* IS REALLY MORE LIKE A BOOK–IT'S NEARLY TWO HUNDRED PAGES LONG AND PERFECT-BOUND. DOES THE DISTINCTION–ZINE OR BOOK–MATTER TO YOU?

This is an answer I've been trying to discover for myself. Throughout the process of writing it, I referred to #5 as a zine. During the very last weeks, I began calling it a book, because I was laying out all those pages, and I think also because it had taken up so much of my attention and energy for so long, I needed to give it more weight. Then, when it finally came back from the printer, I called it a zine, while around me my friends were calling it a book.

I do think that it has elements from both worlds, and may straddle some line between the two. One must then define *book* and *zine,* and I don't think I care to do either.

I like using primary documents in my zines, with no preface or explanation, only the hope that those who read these often tedious papers will gain an understanding of the political complications of a commercial-fishing life. I know many people will skip these documents, which won't affect their greater understanding too terribly much.

I feel that the use of stand-alone primary documents is a very zinelike behavior. I also feel that the fact that I am responsible for all the layout, design, editing, and proofreading is characteristic of zines, as are the resulting numerous typographical errors.

But *Xtra Tuf* #5 reads best if you start on page one and read to the end, which is how most books work. And it does have an ISBN number. Recently my aunt wrote to congratulate me on *XtraTuf* #5, "The Strike Issue," and she added that I should have put my name on the cover. After I read that I turned to my partner, Dwayne, who does a lot of the layout and design with me, and said, "There, my name's not on the cover. It *is* a zine."

I try to maintain a zine ethic, which for me means trading zines with other people and giving them away free to prisoners and commercial fishingwomen, and I write personal letters back to folks who write something beyond, "Here is X dollars. Please send me XXX."

Xtra Tuf #5 costs five dollars from me or at Microcosm, and six dollars elsewhere, which is quite a bit less than a book. People I know who publish their own books seem to pay an awful lot, because they charge an awful lot—twenty-six dollars, twenty-seven dollars for something similar in size and word count to *Xtra Tuf* #5. I don't expect to make money on it—I welcome job offers of either the fishing, writing, or performance kind, which may come from *Xtra Tuf* #5, but I don't really expect money. From the very first issue of *Xtra Tuf*, I thought I would try to pay for postage, that the payoff would come in opening doors and opportunities for me, and it has, far beyond my expectations that summer ten years ago at the Leaky Hovel. But I suspect that may be true for both zines and books.

In the end, I am not sure the distinction matters to me, or more important, to *Xtra Tuf* #5. As my tanner crab crewmate Dave says of such debate, "It is what it is."

MOE'S ASSIGNMENT

one hour

1. Think of a story you tell—a family anecdote, something about a camping trip or prom disaster, some tale of family skeletons—a sitting-around-telling-stories kind of story.

2. Write it down, exactly the way you tell it. Fifteen minutes.

3. Now write it in the present tense. Fifteen minutes.

4. Now write it as a letter to a friend, someone who you know will hang on every word. Indulge their desire to hear all the details. Fifteen minutes.

5. Which one works best?

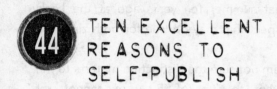

44 TEN EXCELLENT REASONS TO SELF-PUBLISH

I object to publishers: the one service they have done me is to teach me to do without them. They combine commercial rascality with artistic touchiness and pettishness, without being either good businessmen or fine judges of literature. All that is necessary in their production of a book is an author and a bookseller, without the intermediate parasite.

—**George Bernard Shaw**

1. You love books and you want to be a publisher.
2. You need the street cred.
3. You have control issues and need to be in charge of everything from the editing and design to the distribution and promotion of your book.
4. You are dedicated to a DIY philosophy and, come hell or hurricane, you'll do it yourself.
5. Media conglomeration scares you and you don't want anything to do with it.
6. Your audience is small. Say you know your book is only going to sell three to three thousand copies. Just because the audience for a particular book is small, that's no reason not to write it—and it's certainly no reason not to publish it. But a traditional publisher will have a hard time making those numbers work within their business model. With a small self-publishing business model, you can make those numbers work.
7. You want to be a lit star in the tradition of Walt Whitman and Anaïs Nin.

8. You want to make more money. If an outside publisher puts your book out, you'll make roughly a buck a book—or 7 to 10 percent of the cover price—in royalties. With self-publishing, you can set your own royalties—typically 20 to 30 percent of the cover price.
9. Your book has been rejected by fifty agents and fifty publishers and you've decided that . . .
10. You love books and you want to be a publisher.

45 MAKE YOUR OWN BOOKS

So, the first rule of self-publishing is that you do it because you love books and you want to be a publisher. You've got the energy, the heart and guts.

Maybe you've heard about the homeschooled boy wonder Christopher Paolini, or any of a number of other writers with similar stories. It took the fifteen-year-old a year to write his first fantasy novel, *Eragon*. He spent a second year revising the manuscript, and then showed it to his parents. The family decided to self-publish the book, using a print-on-demand service, so they took another year to do edits, design a cover, typeset the manuscript, create the illustrations, and prepare a marketing plan. They set out on a brilliant theatrical tour targeting libraries and high schools across the country and sold the book directly to their target audience. Pretty soon

Alfred A. Knopf got wind of the excitement, bought the rights to publish *Eragon* and the rest of Christopher's *Inheritance* trilogy, and at the age of eighteen, Christopher had himself an international bestseller and an obscene amount of money. The Paolinis did everything right. They put *Eragon* out into the world and the world responded with wild cheers and million-dollar checks. This is not normal. Most self-published books are never picked up by mainstream publishers. Most self-published books, like most books put out by big presses, do not ever hit the *New York Times* bestseller list.

I want you to write, edit, design, copyedit, typeset, lay out, self-publish, and promote your book because you love books, because you *want* to make books, because you think a cross-country tour is just what you need to get out of the rut you're in. I want you to dream big—I want you to have intentions of glory—but I want you to focus on the details of everyday life as a small publisher and remain unattached to the volume of your success. The journey is the destination, man.

Here's the second rule of self-publishing: If anybody sneers and calls it "vanity" publishing, tell them to fuck off. These people are killjoys at best, jealous wannabes at worst.

Many writers choose to self-publish their books because they can't find an established press to do it. For them, the do-it-yourself model is sort of a last resort. This is fine. Many other authors, like Jim Munroe of No Media Kings and Dave Eggers of McSweeney's, found success with top New York houses and *chose* to publish some or all of their subsequent projects themselves because publishing is a difficult, rewarding, glorious process and they wanted to run their own shows.

After frustrating efforts to get her work out into the world in the 1930s, Anaïs Nin bought an old handpress that operated like a sewing machine, with a foot pedal. The man who sold it to her said she could make Christmas cards on it but not fine books. She'd partnered up with an old lover, Gonzalo Moré, who was unemployed and also living in New York at the time. Gonzalo, who loved the world of printing but had no experience, insisted they could make fine books on anything, so Anaïs borrowed some money and rented an attic to house the press.

In January 1942, she wrote in her diary:

> *The press was delivered. We borrowed a book from the library on how to print. Gonzalo would run the press, I would set type. I started to learn typesetting. It took me an hour and a half to typeset half a page. We decided to start with* Winter of Artifice*. . . .*
>
> *The creation of an individual world, an act of independence, such as the work at the press, is a marvelous cure for anger and frustration. The insults of the publishers, the rejections, the ignorance, all are forgotten. I love the studio. I get up with eager curiosity. The press is a challenge. We make mistakes.*

The process of painstakingly typesetting her own work, letter by letter, provided Anaïs with an unexpected lesson in the elegance of concision: "Typesetting slowly makes me analyze each phrase and tighten the style."

She and Gonzalo learned everything they needed to know by trial and error. An eight-hour workday might yield just two pages of type. They learned to print engravings. Sometimes they had to reset entire pages. The press wouldn't work and Gonzalo didn't want to call a workman. He battled with the press. At each stage of the process, they invented, tested, and struggled. "We dreamt, ate, talked, slept with the press. We ate sandwiches with the taste of ink, got ink in our hair and inside our nails."

If you self-publish today, you may or may not choose to actually print the thing yourself. Publishing is not synonymous with printing. Publishing is about preparing the manuscript for its journey into the world—editing it, laying out the pages, and designing a cover. It's about paying a printer or printing it yourself and figuring out a marketing and distribution plan. Click to nomediakings.org for all the information you need to make your own books and put them out via your own indie publishing company. In the meantime, let's talk to Jim Munroe, indie media guru and founder of No Media Kings. . . .

46 VOLUNTEER POWER AND DIRTY GASOLINE

An Interview with Jim Munroe

I first met Jim Munroe in person at the Southwest baggage claim at LAX on Election Day in 2004. The novelist who left HarperCollins to showcase and propagate indie press alternatives to media conglomeration had invited me to come along on "The Perpetual Motion Roadshow." We caught a bus and then a Metro train to meet Richard Melo, author of *Jokerman 8,* and the three of us set off to entertain a string of West Coast audiences suffering from post-election blues. I thought I knew a thing or two about self-promotion, but Jim—almost as famous for shunning everything corporate as for writing excellent sci-fi novels, including *Flyboy Action Figure Comes with Gasmask, Angry Young Spaceman,* and *An Opening Act of Unspeakable Evil*—showed me how it was done. No budget. No rock-star arrogance. Just three writers putting on the best shows they can, and offering work they believe in.

Jim isn't protective of his wisdom; find out how he writes, publishes, distributes, and promotes his work at nomediakings.org. He'll even let you steal his logo. *That anarchist!*

WHAT MADE YOU DECIDE TO LEAVE HARPERCOLLINS AND GO INDIE?

What I learned from my experiences there was that publishing wasn't some kind of black magic. It was a collection of skilled people working together on a project, and through my experiences self-publishing and working in journalism, I had those skills or access to people with those skills. Since I was always uncomfortable with the Rupert Murdoch ownership, and this discomfort never went away, when I thought about my second book, the tantalizing challenge of putting out something with as much polish and media splash as a corporate book became more exciting than staying. So I left, and thanks to an incredible community and a fair amount of hard work, I was able to meet that challenge. My second indie book got more attention and sold better than my first.

THERE'S A PERSISTENT NOTION THAT SELF-PUBLISHED BOOKS JUST AREN'T GOOD ENOUGH FOR "REAL" PUBLISHERS. PLEASE CONFIRM OR DISPEL THIS MYTH.

I've been a voracious and broad reader from a very young age, so I have developed confidence in my taste in writing. I'd been making zines since I was seventeen, and while there's plenty of poorly written stuff out there—or even worse, mediocre stuff that gets attention because the writer is charismatic or quirky—there is a chunk of it that is as good as stuff published by mainstream publishers.

The specter of vanity press is a hard thing to exorcise, even when Shelley, Margaret Atwood, and Dave Eggers have all self-published. I sum it up like this: Twenty years ago the printing mechanics of self-publishing was very difficult, which meant that the people doing it had to be very resourceful . . . or desperate. These days, when we all have professional-quality publishing tools in our home computers, there's a broader spectrum of people getting into self-publishing. I would argue that my generation grew up with zines and indie rock, which are extremely useful models: The zine community allowed me to refine my skills and become a writer in public, and I saw the world gave independent music more artistic credibility.

WHEN I LIST MY PUBLISHING HISTORY ON SOME GRANT APPLICATIONS, I'M NOT ALLOWED TO INCLUDE THINGS I PUBLISHED MYSELF, EVEN THOUGH THEY WERE LEGITIMATE AND GOOD. DO YOU THINK SELF-PUBLISHED WORK WILL START TO BE RECOGNIZED BY ARTS COUNCILS AND OTHER FUNDING GROUPS ANYTIME SOON?

It's kind of like wearing thrift-store clothing. For a long time, if you saw someone wearing thrift clothes, you'd assume they were desperate. Now people thrift for a variety of reasons beyond economic: different era of fashion, dislike of consumerism, etc. Sure, my grandma might still raise her eyebrows when I say I got my cords at Value Village, but most people are hep to the idea that it's become its own thing and valid in its own right. The same thing's happening with self-publishing.

Arts councils, like most institutions, are a little slow to change with the times, but that's pretty understandable and even desirable. I think there's a use for filters and requirements, if just for the reason that it makes the arts councils credible in the eyes of the public—i.e., the funders. What I would propose is a more permeable list of requirements: Spoken-word artists, for instance, can have a list of legit publications or be recognized as a spoken-word artist by their peers. I think something like this should happen in the literary sector as well.

Coverage in the mainstream media could also be considered as another gauge of legitimacy. I think what the councils are using as their filters are a little narrow and could bear expansion.

In some respects, though, a lot of these requirements can already be interpreted quite broadly. For instance, if you were gay, you could insist that your grandma acknowledge it, or you could let her describe you to her friends as a "confirmed bachelor"—old-people code for gay. I think in the case of the arts councils, there's a case for letting it ride sometimes and pushing the issue at others.

I TALK TO A LOT OF FOLKS WHO ARE DRAWN TO SELF-PUBLISHING BUT FEARFUL ABOUT THE PROMOTION SIDE OF THINGS. HOW DO YOU MANAGE TO PROMOTE YOUR OWN WORK? WHY DO YOU THINK THE PROSPECT SCARES NEW AUTHORS?

Promotion is difficult for a lot of people, and if you self-publish you have to be willing to do it. But if you can think about it as a creative act, a kind of theater, then you can use the same muscle in presenting the book to the world that you did in writing it. I personally adapt the material to suit a book launch stage: Instead of reading from my book about teaching English on other planets [*Angry Young Spaceman*], I did a mock infosession with slide show on "Why YOU Should Teach English on Other Planets." For my third book, about Vancouver in the year 2036, I mentioned a lot of corporate brands by name, and since I gave them free advertising in my book, I sent them invoices for product placement. These kinds of stunts get attention and are fun to do. Baiting corporations is not something I would have been able to do easily when I was at HarperCollins, but as an indie I can do anything I feel like.

ON YOUR WEB SITE, YOU MAKE A FINANCIAL ARGUMENT FOR SELF-PUBLISHING. DO YOU REALLY THINK YOU MAKE MORE MONEY PRINTING AND SELLING YOUR OWN BOOKS? HOW DOES THAT WORK?

As the publisher I get a bigger percentage of each book that sells—about five dollars instead of two dollars. Even when my sales numbers are lower, I make as much, if not more. And I never have to worry about the publisher dropping me. Basically, I work harder at it but it's more satisfying.

I DIG HOW YOU INVITE OTHER WRITER-PUBLISHERS TO USE THE NO MEDIA KINGS LOGO FOR THEIR BOOKS. HAVE MANY TAKEN YOU UP ON THAT?

Frank Duff's *Lysergically Yours* was the first book to use it, and it's appeared on zines, CDs, and a short documentary.

Usually what happens is that people get inspired [and plan to use] it, but after they put all the work into it, they come up with their own logo—which makes perfect sense, and the notion is simply that if not having a logo is stopping you, here's one to use.

PLEASE TELL OUR KIND READERS ABOUT "THE PERPETUAL MOTION ROADSHOW"!

"The Perpetual Motion Roadshow" is an indie press touring circuit, an unholy combination of a vaudevillian variety show and a punk rock tour. Each month, three new lively indie performers pile in a car and do seven cities in eight days, doing shows with the bold guarantee: NO BORING

READINGS OR YOUR MONEY BACK! Transnational, it loops the northeast May through October and makes runs down the West Coast during November till April.

Founded by No Media Kings, we've been making our own fun since 2003—running on pure volunteer power and dirty, dirty gasoline.

JIM'S ASSIGNMENT

make a zine

You've probably heard this before, but nothing beats making a zine. You get experience with the whole cycle of publishing; you complete a project and get it out into the world; you meet people who can help you with future projects. Yeah, it's not as impressive to your average person as a slick, corporate book, but you're way more approachable, and thus people are much more inclined to give you feedback. I would say the rate of feedback for my zines was one to ten, where with books it's more like one to one hundred.

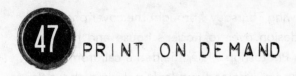

47 PRINT ON DEMAND

In the end, all books are written for your friends.

—**Gabriel Garcia Marquez**

One morning in mid-October I walked into my memoir-writing workshop and asked my students if they'd like to put together an anthology.

Sure! they said.

And so my students got to work polishing their favorite stories and e-mailed them to me by the end of the month. I did some basic editing, arranged them in a way I thought made sense, and put them together into a two-hundred-page Word document. I printed it out, and on the second Sunday in November, we all got together at Lani Jo's house for a proofreading party. The idea was that three readers on each story would catch most of the typos. We had wine and brownies and we each signed off on the stories we read. Once a story had three pairs of initials on it, the writer looked it over to approve the edits and then signed off, too.

I took the pages home and inputted the corrections.

Meanwhile, Linda worked on an interior design, choosing fonts, type size, and leading based on a few good-looking anthologies she found at the library.

I e-mailed her the final manuscript and set about designing a cover.

The following Thursday, I brought the cover photo and the basic design over to Roger's house and he put it together in Photoshop while I fielded a call from one of the contributors, who had suddenly panicked about the unflattering portrait she'd written of her best friend's husband. *Yikes.*

I called Linda and had her change the names and hometowns of the writer's best friend and her husband.

Then Linda formatted the Word document, saved it as a PDF file, and printed it out.

On Friday I headed over to Linda's house and we took a last look at the pages, fixed some typos, double-checked the spelling of everybody's names, and started uploading the thing to the self-publishing site lulu.com. A couple of hours and a few weird computer glitches later, we ordered the first copies of our anthology for ten dollars.

By the end of November everyone could buy a copy of *How to Leave a Place* on lulu.com. We paid an extra $150 for an ISBN number, and it was available on Amazon by Christmas.

Welcome to print-on-demand technology—POD—wherein anyone with ten dollars and a few software programs can publish his own book. Copies are printed only as they are ordered, so the per-book price is more than you'd pay if you went to a traditional offset printer and ordered a thousand copies, but it's less of an investment up front.

A POD book is a great parlor trick for any writer, and an effective, cheap, and hands-free printing and distribution mechanism for serious writers who've developed an audience. The print-on-demand model works best for nonfiction books with a niche audience—preferably one that lives on the Web—but for anyone who wants to self-publish and doesn't have the capital to print a thousand copies right off the bat, it's only a slightly worse system than conventional self-publishing.

If you're considering printing a book using the POD model, keep in mind that you will have to do all of the editing yourself. Lots of books published on iuniverse.com or lulu.com could be great with a little bit of editing, so don't let your excitement stop you from polishing your work. Keep in mind, too, that for a self-published book to get any attention, it needs to get reviewed. The standard number of review copies self-publishers send out to appropriate media is about one hundred, so consider the extra cost of the print-on-demand review copies as you compare the investment and profit potential with that of a traditional self-publishing model.

Whichever route you choose, please accept my heartfelt congratulations. You are about to be a published author!

48 ALL MEDIA AT MY COMMAND

An Interview with Susie Bright

I love Susie Bright—author, editor, performer, educator, mother, and wholly approachable sexual revolutionary. She's been fighting the good fight since most of y'all were shittin' yellow. Born in California in 1958, she began publishing with a homemade pamphlet denouncing then-gubernatorial candidate Ronald Reagan. In orange-red crayons, eight-year-old Susie let the neighborhood know what she thought. She signed the pamphlet "Concerned Citizens of California," and she's been an activist journalist ever since.

The *New York Times* has called her "the avatar of American Erotica." The *Utne Reader* dubbed her "one of the leading thinkers and visionaries of our time." The *Los Angeles Reader* noted that she's "the least pretentious, most down-to-earth cultural revolutionary you'd ever want to meet." And the late Andrea Dworkin famously called her "a reactionary woman hater."

She first started writing about sex in the early eighties in San Francisco and in 1984 cofounded and edited *On Our Backs: Entertainment for the Adventurous Lesbian*. The founding editor of *Herotica*—erotica written by women—and editor of *The Best American Erotica,* she also teaches The Politics of Sexual Representation—or Porn 101.

For all Susie's advice on writing and publishing, click on over to susiebright.com and get a copy of her book *How to Write a Dirty Story.* The reigning queen of contemporary erotica will teach you how to heat up your sex scenes in any genre. "I want more people to write frankly about sex," she writes in the book's intro. "I want to see an end to erotic illiteracy and to the censorship of sexual speech. I want to gut the stupidity and stereotypes that surround so many public discussions of sex and art." Her many other books include *Susie Sexpert's Lesbian Sex World, Full Exposure: Opening Up to Sexual Creativity and Erotic Expression,* and *Mommy's Little Girl: On Sex, Motherhood, Porn, and Cherry Pie.*

I'M WRITING A BOOK ABOUT HOW TO BECOME A FAMOUS WRITER BEFORE YOU'RE DEAD.

I could do a book about how to become a famous but utterly broke writer before you're dead.

I KNOW. MY DAUGHTER IS WORKING AT TACO TIME AND SHE MAKES MORE MONEY THAN I DO.

Tell it like it is, sister! Taco Time, here I come!

OKAY. YOU WERE FAMOUS BEFORE YOUR FIRST BOOK CAME OUT, RIGHT?

You're funny. I would not say I'm well known outside certain circles.

My first book was something I edited, *Herotica,* in 1987. I started *On Our Backs* in 1984 with my friends.

I was performing and being out there with various renegades in the early eighties. But my FBI file goes back to high school, when I was involved in an underground high-school newspaper with ties to Wounded Knee, the Panthers, the antiwar movement, early labor stuff, etc. So I was famous with certain esoteric elements for a while. Hell, I was Goldilocks, the star of the kindergarten play in 1964. True, true fame!

I think my name became interesting to people in the mid-eighties, because of *On Our Backs.*

BUT YOU FIRST BROKE INTO PUBLISHING WHEN YOU WERE STILL IN HIGH SCHOOL.

Yes. The high-school newspaper was called *The Red Tide,* in Los Angeles, in the seventies. We did it all. That's how I learned newspaper production. I was a commie, a feminist, and a poet, and we always had a million things we wanted to print to influence the world!

NOW YOU'VE PUBLISHED THE MAGAZINE, BOOKS WITH BIG PRESSES AND BOOKS WITH SMALL PRESSES, DONE AN E-BOOK. . . . HAVE YOU SELF-PUBLISHED BOOKS?

Yes. I self-published *How to Read/Write a Dirty Story,* which then got picked up by a publisher and reissued as *How to Write a Dirty Story.* I've also published my own e-books.

AND YOU HAVE YOUR WEB SITE AT SUSIEBRIGHT.COM, YOUR MOST EXCELLENT BLOG. . . . I DIG HOW YOU JUST GET YOUR STUFF OUT THERE. WHAT ARE SOME OF THE PROS

AND CONS OF THE DIFFERENT PUBLISHING VEHICLES YOU'VE USED?

Well, now when I think back on it, I don't know how we ever scraped two dimes together to pay the printing press. And we had to wait so long to see the fruits of our labors. With my blog, it's just write, take a breath, and post. And my publishing overhead is in the three figures per month, not five figures.

What's different about books, of course, and magazines is the whole sensual experience of paper and binding and holding it in your hands, and its legacy and its huge, huge accessibility. The blogosphere feels like it's everyone, but it's really the most insane elite.

I would love to print books and magazines. It's money that stops me, nothing else. I would ideally like to have all media at my command—who wouldn't?

WHAT DOES YOUR WORKDAY AND WORKWEEK LOOK LIKE?

It's deadline driven. It's never the same. I binge and purge. My best hours are in the morning, brain-wise. I don't work well at night.

DO YOU REQUIRE YOURSELF TO WRITE FOR A CERTAIN TIME PERIOD EACH DAY?

When I have a book deadline looming, yes. One chapter per day or die. Otherwise, no.

WHAT ABOUT THE CASH FLOW?

The endless subtraction.

SUSIE'S ASSIGNMENT

fantasies

Give yourself two minutes to answer each of the following questions. When your time is up, stop, even if you haven't finished your sentence.

- Write down an erotic fantasy about a sexual experience that you would have in a minute if it were offered to you, no questions asked. It should be something you would have no reservations or conditions about doing in real life.
- Write down an erotic fantasy about a sexual experience that you would only have under certain conditions. You could give yourself up wholeheartedly under these conditions, but otherwise not at all.
- Write down an erotic fantasy about a sexual experience that is completely satisfying to you in your imagination but that you could not do because it is either physically impossible or something you could never bring yourself to do in real life. . . . Yet in your mind, it is completely hot and fulfilling.

Now you have three potential pieces of fiction, based on your fantasies. Take another sheet of paper and answer the following:

- What do you notice about the differences, or similarities, between your three fantasies?
- Have you ever confided any of these fantasies to anyone?
- Is any one of your three fantasies more compelling than another, sexually or creatively?

After you finish this exercise, you'll never believe again . . .

- That your fantasy life is barren.
- That fantasies can only be satisfied by acting them out.
- That fantasies are not enhanced by conflicts, taboos, and inhibitions. (Like literature, they thrive on all those things!)

49 BLOG THIS

I'm a print girl. I'll always have a soft place in my heart for newspapers and zines and little folded notes passed between desks. Given the choice, I would always rather walk into a real bookstore, pick up a real book and hold it in my hands, pay cash for it. Don't make me download a whole novel.

But clicking around the Internet with my high-speed connection is so quick! So easy! I discover writers I never would have found in my local independent bookstore, never would have taken a chance on if I had to shell out real money on that first encounter.

Publishing a little zine takes all afternoon—and that's if you're superhero fast. It usually takes me a good three months to get an issue of *Hip Mama* out the door. Another month in the bulk mail if you subscribe. It's worth the wait. A book takes even longer. Even if you've written the whole thing, it'll take a publisher a year to get it out into the world. It's worth the wait, too. But I can publish online right this very second. There's no time for shame-spiraling and no time for news to get old. Instant gratification. I can write a poem at noon, post it on my Web site at noon, e-mail my grandmother and all my friends directing them to the new material at noon, and someone out there in the world might just read my poem at noon. Even better, it's free. Well, it's not quite free if you want to have your own computer and your own Internet connection and maybe even some fancy-pants to design your Web site . . . but it *can* be free. Just go to blogger.com and get started. Maybe hordes of fans will be drawn immediately to your site or maybe it'll take some time to get the word out, but your stories will instantly be available to the whole world of online folks.

Blogging can be fun. Some folks even make money at it. And lots of bloggers are able to quickly disseminate important information—they blog from high-school libraries and prisons; from Beijing and Baghdad. Notes passed between desks aren't always adequate. Sometimes we don't have time to wait for the printer. So get to blogging. Get your first works out into the world. If you're writing news, get it out there now. And if you're writing poetry, get it out there! These things can't wait. William Carlos Williams said, "It is difficult to get the news from poems yet men die miserably every day for lack of what is found there."

Nourish the world with your words, yo.

50 ASK MAGNIFICENT METEOR

Rising Lit Star asks: Okay. Where do I start? I'm a hospital worker and a yoga teacher. I've been furiously scribbling in a journal and writing on friends' blogs for ages and have no frigging idea what to do with my jewels. I wanna write. I do.

Magnificent Meteor reveals: Sounds like you're already writing. Now join a writing workshop or start a writing group. Go out to open mics and read your jewels. It's time for you to move from journaling to writing for strangers. Taking a ten-week workshop will give you a structure and a weekly deadline and get you accustomed to sharing your work with an intimate group. Going to open mics will help you with the performance side of writing and motivate you to write more. Then start putting your stuff out in a humble zine—send it to friends and strangers, advertise it on your friends' blogs, send it to zine-review zines, put it out on consignment in your local indie bookstores.

Rising Lit Star asks: What should I be doing now? Writing for zines? Submitting stuff to bigger-name shiny magazines? Writing stuff for someone's anthology? Seducing semi-important people for my book deal? Finishing college so I sound like I know what I'm talking about?

Magnificent Meteor reveals: Yes on the first three. Absolutely! The last two aren't important unless you're enjoying yourself doing it.

Rising Lit Star asks: How can I make a living from poetry?

Magnificent Meteor reveals: Print poetry on sexy T-shirts and sell them on the Internet.

Rising Lit Star asks: How do I know if others will want to read what I write? Am I just fooling myself that my writing is readable?

Magnificent Meteor reveals: Publish a zine and find out. If no one wants to read it yet, you just need more practice, so keep publishing the zine.

Rising Lit Star asks: How do I find a good editor?

Magnificent Meteor reveals: If you need an editor because you are planning to self-publish or because your manuscript isn't ready for an agent or an outside publisher, you've got two options:

1. Pay someone. Ask around among your writer acquaintances. Find someone with book-editing experience and references. You should be able to find an editor who'll give your manuscript a basic edit for two hundred dollars to five hundred dollars.

2. Join a writing workshop or convene a writing group in which you will be able to bring a chapter a week for feedback (if it's a workshop, check with the instructor to make sure this will work given the format of the class). A workshop of about eight to ten people will get you some whack feedback—don't let a committee get you to toss the deep shit that makes your writing yours—but a group that size will also be able to give you a good collective edit. People will call

you on the stuff you know is problematic but were hoping you could get away with, they'll be able to point out confusing bits or places where they want more details, and they'll find a lot of the typos.

PART FOUR

play with the big dogs

And it does no harm to repeat, as often as you can, "Without me the literary industry would not exist: the publishers, the agents, the sub-agents, the sub-sub-agents, the accountants, the libel lawyers, the departments of literature, the professors, the theses, the books of criticism, the reviewers, the book pages—all this vast and proliferating edifice is because of this small, patronized, put-down and underpaid person."

—Doris Lessing

51 BE NICE TO INTERNS

You should be nice to interns at newspapers, magazines, and publishing houses because they work hard and don't get paid. You should be nice to interns because they are people, just like you. Here's another reason you should be nice to interns: Interns become publicists become editors. That's just the way it works. You rip an intern a new asshole today and not only does she turn around and tell her boss what a jerk you are, but you bungle a sale that would have taken place five years down the road. Editors remember when they were interns.

I can't tell you how many times I've gotten a nasty e-mail in the *Hip Mama* in-box, only to respond myself and get some long-winded apology about how the nasty one never would have been so nasty if she'd known it was "really me" on the other end of the computer. *Excuse me? So you just thought you'd ruin some peon's day?*

E-mail access makes impulsive, hotheaded letter-writing easier than ever. You don't need a stamp. You don't need to wait until you've sobered up. You don't need to wait for the mail carrier. If you are prone to bitchiness—or to getting drunk or manic and sending out e-mails and then shame-spiraling in the morning—learn to hand-write your venting rants and save them. If they still look righteous and important in the light of morning, type them up, send them off, and learn to live with the consequences.

52 HOW TO PISS OFF AN EDITOR

© Ariel Gore

I love to get a submission envelope adorned with fancy stickers and mad-happy doodles. This is why I'm a zine editor and don't have a job at a highbrow literary mag. But unless you're damn sure your submissions editor likes puffy googly-eye stickers, leave them off. See, editors are a persnickety lot, each with his own pet peeves and soft spots, but there are a few things editors find so universally annoying as to guarantee you a spot in the recycling bin.

This font, for example, is poison to your literary career. No one wants to see this font unless they're getting an invitation to a free gourmet lunch on a yacht.

Use a simple serif font like twelve-point Times New Roman. The look you're going for is classic, elegant . . . *plain.*

Your manuscript should be on standard-weight white paper. No lavender card stock. No perfumed stationery. Use one-inch margins and double-space. Indent your paragraphs and don't add an extra space between them. We're in the age of computers now, not typewriters, so you only need one space after a period, not two. Staple your story in the upper left-hand corner and include your contact information on the first page. Cover letters often get lost, and I've still got a great story sitting here next to my desk with no clue as to who wrote it, so include your contact info, but don't include the little copyright symbol. It says to an editor: "I think this story is so good and I think you're so evil that you're going to steal it from me and not give me the million bucks it's worth." And that's not a very nice how-do-you-do, is it? If you're paranoid that some editor is going to steal your story, that's fine, but be privately paranoid. You can stick a copy of your story in a manila envelope, mail it to yourself, and leave it unopened. The postmark will prove to any judge when you wrote it. If you're more paranoid still, send a copy to the Library of Congress. But leave the little copyright symbol off your submission.

53 MEET YOUR DEADLINES

> A deadline is negative inspiration. Still, it's better than no inspiration at all.
>
> —**Rita Mae Brown**

Remember what my professor Sarah Pollock said? "It isn't the most talented writer in this room who will be the most widely published, it's the one who meets her deadlines." From that moment, I never missed a deadline. Okay, maybe I missed one, but it was for an anarchist magazine whose editor didn't know what day it was. What do you do at eleven P.M. on the night of your midnight deadline? You lower your standards. Make a mad dash to the finish line. Any widely published writer who tells you that deadlines don't matter is either lying or she's a lot more talented than you are. Deadlines matter. Obviously, you don't want to get into the habit of delivering mediocre work—that's not going to do you any good in the long run—but you'll notice that if you force yourself to meet your deadlines, you'll learn to produce better and better writing in whatever amount of time you have. You'll master the sprint as well as the marathon.

Meet your deadlines. Meet them every time. An editor can forgive a real emergency, but if you've left someone with a blank page in their publication the night before they were supposed to go to press, it better be a damn good emergency. Something usable tonight is always better than something great tomorrow. As the fisherman R. Blondin quoted in *Xtra Tuf* says, "There's the A list, the B list, and the shit list."

Better to be on the B list than the shit list.

54 SIZE MATTERS

A standard book is about 60,000 words, or 250 pages. Anything under 45,000 words is a novella. Anything over 80,000 or 90,000 words edges toward epic. If you're writing a book and hope to get it published, shoot for about 60,000 words. Novellas are rarely published here now in America. Cheesecake-thick tomes, while somewhat more marketable than novellas, are also fairly hard sells. The price of paper is one of a publisher's biggest expenses. Do they want to take a chance on little old you? Maybe. But if it's going to cost them twice as much as it would cost them to take a chance on me, well, yours better be a masterpiece.

With an article or a short story, length requirements vary from market to market, but generally you are going to want to write between 800 and 5,000 words. Anything under 800 words is filler; anything over 5,000 words is going to take up too much space in the publication. Study your markets. Count words. You'll find standards in most magazines and journals.

Once you're an established lit star, you'll be able to get away with all kinds of things—600-page books and 130-page books; 200-word stories and 7,000-word stories—but here's something you'll probably never get away with: a 50-page story. Ah, the plight of the 50-page story. Too long to be a short story, too short to be a real book. *What is it?* I'll tell you what it is: It's a little something you are going to self-publish as your first—*what shall we call it?*—chapbook. If you don't want to self-publish, stay away from the 50-page story.

55 THE POSSIBILITY OF DISASTER

An Interview with Dave Eggers

In case you spent the turn of the millennium under a log, I'll quickly recap the staggering career of Dave Eggers: His debut memoir, *A Heartbreaking Work of Staggering Genius,* was a finalist for the Pulitzer Prize, a *New York Times Book Review* Editor's Choice, and was named "Best Book of the Year" by the *Los Angeles Times, San Francisco Chronicle, Washington Post,* and *Time.* The shaggy-headed little zine publisher had made the big time. He followed up with the novel *You Shall Know Our Velocity!* and *How We Are Hungry.*

Dave routinely works with mainstream publishers, but he's never been content to leave all the publishing up to anybody else. In 1998 he founded McSweeney's, an independent publisher of books, a quarterly literary journal, *The Believer,* and a daily humor Web site. In 2002 he opened 826 Valencia, a writing lab for young people in the Mission District of San Francisco, where he teaches writing to high-school students and runs a summer publishing camp. With the help of his workshop students, Eggers edits a collection of fiction, essays, and journalism called *The Best American Nonrequired Reading.*

I don't know Dave personally, but I'd heard that he only did interviews via e-mail—either because he's shy or because he wants a paper trail—so I sent a note to his Web site.

GREETINGS MR. EGGERS-

MY NAME IS ARIEL GORE. I DO THE ZINE *HIP MAMA* & AM WORKING ON A NEW BOOK ABOUT THE CREATIVE PROCESS & HOW TO BECOME A FAMOUS WRITER BEFORE YOU'RE DEAD. AND SINCE YOU ARE FAMOUS AND NOT DEAD, I WAS WONDERING IF I COULD TROUBLE YOU FOR A BRIEF INTERVIEW. WHAT DO YOU SAY?

Hey Ariel Gore,
I was just forwarded your note about the book about writing and not being dead. I feel like I mighta contributed to too many books for aspiring writers—so you may not want me in yours, which I assume'll be better than the rest. But let me know what them questions you have are. If I can think of anything interesting to say, I'd be proud to be in anything with your name on it.

OH, COME ON. SHARE THE LOVE FOR ONE MORE. IT'LL BE BETTER THAN THE REST, AND I REALLY NEEDED THE ADVANCE. QUESTION NUMBER ONE: HOW DO YOU MAKE A READING UNBORING?

I used to just try to hand off the readings to other, more interesting people. I would always bring along a whale expert, or a former FBI super-agent, or an expert on toxic-waste disposal. In Kansas City and Minneapolis, I did a series of panels about itching. I just would rather watch something unexpected happen than just have me read the same things. But these days the readings I do are more straightforward. It took too much time to get those more elaborate readings together, and of course there was always the possibility of disaster, which keeps you up at night before—and long after—the events.

HOW DO YOU BALANCE WHAT APPEARS FROM AFAR TO BE A BIT OF SHY INTROVERSION WITH GETTING THE ATTENTION YOU NEED TO SUPPORT YOUR WORK? DO YOU HAVE A SUPERHERO ALTER EGO?

The only thing we've ever done at McSweeney's, in terms of getting attention for our books, is to post stuff on our Web site. And then we send the books out to people.

ABOUT HOW MANY REVIEW COPIES DO YOU SEND OUT ON AVERAGE?

Anywhere from thirty for a smaller book to about two hundred for something we're thinking might sell better.

We've never had a budget for ads or other PR gambits. This past year, we hired someone to actually handle publicity for the books, but it turned out we couldn't afford it. So we're back to our staff of four, just mailing out books and hoping for the best.

HAS YOUR EXPERIENCE PUBLISHING MAGAZINES AND ZINES AND BOOKS—AND DOING PROMOTION AND DISTRIBUTION STUFF—MADE YOU MORE OR LESS EMPATHETIC TO INDUSTRY BIGHEADS?

More empathetic, for the most part. We've had lots of good experiences with big publishing companies. We do benefit books for 826 Valencia, and for these we need big-publisher cooperation, since McSweeney's doesn't have the muscle to sell mass quantities of anything—like the genre collection that Michael Chabon did for 826, *Thrilling Tales*. So we worked with Geoff Kloske when he was at Simon & Schuster, and he was pretty much a saint, and Marty Asher at Vintage, who was always very cool about doing things in different ways. We also work with Houghton Mifflin on *The Best American Nonrequired Reading*. For the most part, we've been lucky, in that the people at these companies are just regular, good book people. By and large, the book business, at whatever level, is still a pretty polite and good-hearted entity. And we know really well how narrow the profit margins are on books, so the fact that some of these companies are even staying in business is baffling to me. It's really, really hard to make a dime on a book selling less than ten thousand copies, and unfortunately, the majority of McSweeney's books land in that category. Which is why we work out of a one-bedroom apartment in the Mission.

DAVE'S ASSIGNMENT

hard bound

I think one of the most useful things to do is—if and after you've written what you want to write—put your work between covers, do-it-yourself style. I started making hardcover books when I was eleven, and it always gives you a sense of legitimacy, and even permanence. So take your stories or novel, use Quark or PageMaker or InDesign to lay them out the way you'd like them to be, print them, cut the pages to a standard 5½-by-8½-inch format, and have a copy shop do a glue binding on the stack. Then wrap a cover around it—rip one off an existing book if you need to—do your own dust jacket, and hold the object in your hands. Suddenly your work will feel more real than before, I bet, and if you're struggling to get that work published, or procrastinating with it, holding that sample in your hands can be the jet fuel you need to continue.

56 DON'T SUBMIT BLINDLY TO PUBLISHED AUTHORS

I just heard yet another editor tell yet another group of developing writers that they should submit their manuscripts to established authors in the hopes of getting an agent referral. *What is this?* Can the editors and the agents not get interns? Now they want to push their slush piles off onto us, the already-underpaid slaves of the publishing industry? How tacky!

I mean, it's totally okay to write to published authors. It's okay to write them fan mail, ask for advice, request some kind of mentorship—anything. You needn't be intimidated by a writer just because she's got her name on a book. If an author has changed your life or helped you through a rough time or made you appreciate a rock sparrow's call, by all means introduce yourself and say so. A lot of writers don't get enough feedback. And some don't get much mail. But please don't take it personally if an author doesn't respond. Most of us don't have assistants. Some of my most treasured fan mail, I'm embarrassed to say, has gone unanswered. And writers who are strangers to you are not going to be able to help you much. They probably don't have time to read your manuscript. They're busy selling the freebie author copies of their own books down at the used-book store for money to put some tortellini on the table.

If you're out and about—taking classes, going to writers' workshops and a few conferences, getting internships at new and established literary journals, submitting to anthologies, trading zines, talking to folks on the Internet, hosting open mics, and touring around a bit—you will soon know other writers. And soon after that you'll know published authors. Folks in your own writing community will start to find success. *Those* are the authors who can help you out. People you already know and people with whom you've developed a relationship of mutual help.

If you were once a student of mine, if we read each other's livejournals, if we've exchanged e-mails or zines about this or that, I am happy to read ten pages of your manuscript and rack my brain for an editor or an agent who might be able to help you. But if you're a total stranger to me and you send me your three-hundred-page single-spaced manuscript fresh from Kinko's, it's going to go unread. I'm glad you sent it—you're bold, and bold is never a bad thing—but I won't read it. I can't. I have to go pick my daughter up from the late shift at Taco Time. I have to finish *this* book. I have six unpaid bills on my kitchen table. I have to take the dogs for a walk lest they relieve themselves in my laundry pile. It's nothing personal—it's just the last thing on my to-do list. And as we learned in Chapter 1, no one ever does the last thing on her to-do list.

57 REVEL IN REJECTION

> If every agent in the end turns you down, you will know you're either not good enough or too good. If you're too good, keep writing, and keep your contacts with the writing community available to you, and eventually your day will come.
>
> —**John Gardner**

Dr. Seuss's first book, *To Think That I Saw It on Mulberry Street,* was rejected by dozens of publishers before he finally got a friend to publish it—probably out of pity. Joseph Heller's *Catch-22* was rejected twenty-one times before publication. It's said that Gertrude Stein wrote and kept on submitting poems for twenty-two years before one was accepted. Octavia Butler's classic *Kindred* was repeatedly rejected by publishers, many of whom couldn't understand how a science fiction novel could be set on a plantation in the South. Other classics famously and repeatedly rejected: *War and Peace, The Good Earth, Watership Down, The Tale of Peter Rabbit, The Postman Always Rings Twice, The Fountainhead, To Kill a Mockingbird, Remembrance of Things Past,* and *Joy of Cooking.* Doris Lessing was once rejected by her own publishers when she submitted a novel under a pseudonym. And, in early 2006, the *Sunday Times* of London took two Booker Prize–winning novels—one by V. S. Naipaul and one by Stanley Middleton—and submitted them as works by aspiring authors. None of the agents or editors queried recognized the manuscripts as prizewinners from the 1970s, and of the twenty-one replies, all but one were rejections. A single literary agent, Barbara Levy, expressed an interest in Middleton's novel, but she was unimpressed with Naipaul's. "We . . . thought it was quite original," she wrote. "In the end though I'm afraid we just weren't quite enthusiastic enough to be able to offer to take things further."

All this to say that if you get a rejection slip, you're in pretty good company.

Sometimes you'll get a rejection letter because your story is amateurish and uninteresting. Maybe you wrote that your father was a really good cook when what you meant to do was invite us to the dinner table and feed us buttery cilantro grilled corn and spicy chipotle drumsticks. But often a rejection letter says nothing about a story and even less about you. Dr. Seuss, Octavia Butler, Naipaul, or Lessing would have gotten the same response.

A form rejection letter can mean the story never got read. Or it can mean that it didn't match the publication's unannounced theme for the season. It can mean that you've got a traditionally male name and the editors are looking for more female writers. Or it can mean that the intern had a bad night and your voice reminds him of his ex. Don't put any stock in a form rejection letter; simply send a thank-you note telling whoever signed it that you appreciate their time.

The personalized rejection letter, anything from a form rejection letter with an extra sentence or two thrown in to an actual critique of your work—now, this is something potentially helpful. Sometimes the note is just a courtesy, but if the comment rings true or if you get similar comments from several submissions editors, it may be valuable feedback, one way or another. Jean Cocteau said, "Listen carefully to first criticisms of your work. Note just what it is about your work that the critics don't like—then cultivate it. That's the part of your work that's individual and worth keeping."

And, because capitalism knows no limits, you can

actually upload the text of a rejection letter you get from a publisher and, for ninety dollars, Lulu.com will print it on four rolls of toilet paper for your wiping needs.

58 WHEN DESTINY CALLS

An Interview with Bertice Berry

Bertice Berry grew up poor—the sixth of seven kids—and was told by a teacher that she "wasn't college material." Of course, that teacher is eating her words now. Bertice graduated magna cum laude from Jacksonville University in Florida, was awarded the President's Cup for leadership, and went on to earn a Ph.D. in sociology from Kent State. Using humor to address serious subjects in her lectures, Dr. Berry became one of that university's most popular teachers.

In the early 1990s, Dr. Berry took her show on the road—left Kent State to become an award-winning entertainer, lecturer, and comedian. She won the national Comedian of the Year Award and was named Campus Lecturer of the Year and Campus Entertainer of the Year. She even hosted her own nationally syndicated talk show, *The Bertice Berry Show.*

"When you walk in purpose," she says, "you collide with destiny."

Berry's first books were works of nonfiction: the best-selling inspirational memoir *I'm on My Way, But Your*

Foot Is on My Head, Sckraight from the Ghetto: You Might Be Ghetto If . . ., and its sequel, *You Still Ghetto: You Know You're Still Ghetto If. . . .* As an artist and a human, she's ever-evolving. For the new millennium, she turned to fiction, publishing four novels in six years: *Redemption Song, The Haunting of Hip Hop, Jim & Louella's Home-made Heart-fix Remedy,* and *When Love Calls, You Better Answer.* In these warm and complex stories, ancestors guide the living, everyday magic has the power to transform lives, and harsh truths are brewed into elixirs of hope.

"Instant mother" to her sister's four kids and co-owner of Iona's Gallery, an exhibition space and community center, Dr. Berry lives in Savannah, Georgia.

AS WRITERS, WE ALL HAVE TO DEAL WITH REJECTION. DO YOU HAVE ANY WISDOM THAT MIGHT HELP US HANDLE IT BETTER?

I grew up really poor. My family lived in an alley. So you're already primed for rejection. As a result, I really haven't had to face much. If somebody said to me, "I don't really like this—how about something else?" I didn't take that as rejection. When you've been through a lot, you're very prepared.

I have a wonderful and honest agent. And sometimes when I give her an idea and there isn't any response—just the sound of the crickets—I say, All right, well, how about this other thing?

I went out on a date with a man who called me back right away and said, "I can't believe I'm so attracted to you!"

I said, "Why can't you believe it?"

He said, "I'm usually attracted to people who are thinner."

I said, "Well, I'm usually attracted to people with more money."

Now, there was a time when I might have taken that differently. But what he said wasn't about me. It was about him.

I wrote what I thought was my best book, and that's the only one Random House didn't want to publish. They said it was a good book and well-written, but it wasn't what my audience expected from me. So I wrote another book. I had to sit down and take off my little ego. What they were saying was that my readers weren't ready for it. And my role is not to frighten people, it's to inspire and uplift. You have to get people to a place where they can hear you. Sometimes our reaction to rejection is not admitting that people are right.

Later, after *The Da Vinci Code* came out and I said, That's just like my book, only it's in the fourteenth century and it's in Italy, they said, All right, why don't you go back and edit that book. While I was researching, I found the man who owned the plantation my family worked on. I had always said they were slaves, and there was this horrible man. Well, I finally found him in my research. It turns out he was the southernmost conductor of the Underground Railroad. In Delaware. He led people out, including Harriet Tubman. So that "no" led me to this new book. That "no" was a "yes" to something else.

IN YOUR NOVELS, THE LIVING ARE GUIDED BY THEIR ANCESTORS. HOW ARE YOU GUIDED IN YOUR WRITING?

Because I'm a sociologist, because I'm a statistician, I really like to be in control, but as a writer, you're not in control. I start with an outline. I start with a working title. I do a lot of research—it sounds like homespun wisdom, but it comes from research, from sociological journals. And then I just listen. Once I start hearing the characters' voices, they are my guides. My last book—the ending was a surprise—I was like, *Oh my God!* You have to swing between the left and the right brain at all times.

I'VE TALKED TO SOME ASPIRING AUTHORS WHO FEEL COMFORTABLE WRITING STORIES AND POEMS AND ARTICLES, BUT WHEN IT COMES TO WRITING A BOOK-ESPECIALLY WITH THE AIM OF PUBLISHING IT WITH A BIG PRESS-THERE IS AN INTERNALIZED CLASSISM. SOMETIMES PEOPLE FEEL THAT THE WORK OF AUTHORING BOOKS BELONGS TO AN ELITIST CLASS THEY AREN'T A PART OF.

I remember being at a meeting for my first book—it was an inspirational memoir—and this guy said, "You haven't lived long enough to write an autobiography." I said, "It's not an autobiography, it's an inspirational memoir, but thank you." That kind of arrogance is not where I live. I grew up in an alley. I was told I wasn't college material. I got my Ph.D. at twenty-six. Everybody doesn't know what you need to know. Throughout life, if we are people who are evolving, we will always feel marginal to something. You will feel marginalized from the hood that you came from. You will feel marginalized from the world you are moving into.The classism and the racism and the sexism is there, but it was there when my mother had to feed seven kids by herself—and she did it.

What I see published is what people think they can sell. When I came [to the book publishing industry] from television, I thought, *Surely these are the people who will be more concerned with substance.* Well, no. They want something they can sell.

There are two books that will sell: a great story told and a story told greatly. You can have two brothers who go fishing, or you can have a guy who takes pictures of bridges and has an affair—those aren't great stories, but they can be told greatly. Or you can have *The Color Purple*. That is a great story. And it didn't have to be told in a highfalutin way.

Sometimes people have to get past their own ego to do what they are here to do. If you have a story to tell, then tell it. That said, if I had a quarter for everybody who thinks they should write a book, I'd be on the beach. That's not fair. That's not fair to the people who put their heart and soul into writing. Be who you were put here to be, and if that includes telling a story, tell that story. You have to find the strength to go beyond all the other junk they throw at you.

BERTICE'S ASSIGNMENTS

focus on the right agents

To find an agent, look at the books you like. Agents now have gotten to a place where they can specialize. So look at the books you like and are like yours and read the acknowledgments. We all tend to thank our agents. So narrow your focus to those agents. Find the folks who do what you want to do, and your rejection will be a lot less. Often rejection is just, "That's not what I do."

go longhand

Computers are not second nature to me. Write a chapter longhand. You will find it much easier. The brain is wired to the rest of the body—not to the laptop. So try writing longhand—you don't edit as much. You allow that guiding to happen.

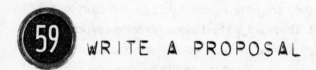

59 WRITE A PROPOSAL

It's easier to sell a nonfiction book such as a how-to guide, a self-help manual, or an informational volume on a subject with a known audience—like, say, home improvement or nutrition—than it is to sell a novel, a literary memoir, or a poetry collection. People buy more books on how to build a cobhouse or lose a hundred pounds over the weekend than they do lyrical explorations of one young woman's relationship with her alcoholic mother. That's just the way it is.

If you're a budding novelist, you needn't jump the fence just because the grass is greener, but it is. Undeniably. Greener. To get an agent—and then a publisher—for a nonfiction book, you don't even have to write the whole thing. You just have to write a proposal detailing what you'll write if they pay you.

Novels are sold only after you've got the whole book written. However! Every novelist would do well to write a faux proposal—a summary of the story and the marketing strategy. With fiction, it can be difficult to focus on what the book is "about," but it's important to be able to sum it up when you want to sell it to agents and editors, and again when you want to promote it to the larger reading audience.

A standard proposal includes a title page, the proposal contents (i.e., what you're including in the proposal), an introduction, a full table of contents for the book you're going to write, a one-page author bio highlighting your writing credits and unique qualification to write this book, a one-page analysis of competitive titles that shows how your book is going to stand out from others on the same subject, a one-page marketing plan, a brief statement on the format of the book and the length of time you'll need to complete it, and three sample chapters. Some folks insist that the three sample chapters have to be the *first* three chapters, but I've never had any trouble submitting just the first chapter and then a few random excerpts. The proposal for this book, for instance, included the introduction and one chapter from each section.

The length of a book proposal can vary depending on your subject matter and your track record as a writer. As a rule, the fewer writing credits you have, the more substantial your proposal will have to be. The proposal for my first book, *The Hip Mama Survival Guide,* was eighty pages. The proposal for this book was a brief twenty. I had to give editors a clear idea of the finished project I had in mind, but because I've written other successful books, I didn't have to spend time convincing anyone that I could, in fact, complete a manuscript.

When you're ready to get started on your proposal, pick up a copy of Michael Larsen's Writers Digest classic *How to Write a Book Proposal*—he'll lead you through the process as you summarize your book and life into a nice industry-standard proposal. When you've got it just about right, stick it in an envelope, light a good-luck candle, and send your proposal off to agents or directly to an editor you have reason to believe will be interested. And sit tight.

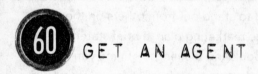

60 GET AN AGENT

> You must keep sending work out; you must never let a manuscript do nothing but eat its head off in a drawer. You send that work out again and again, while you're working on another one. If you have talent, you will receive some measure of success—but only if you persist.
>
> —**Isaac Asimov**

If you want to publish with a big house, you're going to need an agent. Agents help publishers by weeding out the mediocre stuff and agents help writers by having connections to the right editors, packaging our manuscripts, negotiating our contracts, collecting our money, and sort of babysitting us through the prepublishing process. In return, an agent gets 15 percent of our advances and royalties. You don't pay an agent anything up front, they work solely on commission, so if they don't think they can sell your book, they're not going to waste time on it. But if they think they can get a six-figure advance, they're going to invest some time with you and earn a pretty penny for their trouble.

As Bertice Berry suggests, target agents by looking at the acknowledgments pages of books you like and books that are similar to yours. Authors tend to thank their agents. Then Google the name to get contact information. If the agent or agency has a Web site, read everything on it—especially the submissions guidelines. Don't submit by e-mail unless you find specific instructions to do so. Don't send your whole manuscript unless the agent asks for it. Send a query letter and up to ten sample pages of your book. Your query letter should be brief—no more than a page—and include:

- Your contact info
- The agent's name (spelled correctly!)
- A request that the agent read your manuscript
- A mention of where you got the agent's name
- The title of your book

- A brief summary of the book's genre and story
- Mention of a couple of similar titles the agent has successfully represented
- Your publishing credits (your best three to five are enough)
- A thank you
- A sign-off

That's it. A query, like a cover letter, should be formatted like a business letter—single-spaced with extra spaces in between the paragraphs. So your query should look something like this:

Future Lit Star
P.O. Box 1000
Great Town, CA
90000
Litstar@hotmail.com
555-323-5220

Dear Fabulous Agent,

I am writing in hopes you'll be interested in reading my novel, *Chasing the Immortal Peach*. It is contemporary women's fiction and tells the story of a young runaway in San Francisco in the early 1970s. With your success with novels like Annie Silver's *New York Street-Punk* and Joe Martin's *Sailing East*, I think this might be a good fit for your list.

I'm the editor/publisher of the zine *Runaway* (circulation 10,000), my short stories have appeared in Some

Literary Journal, and I won third place in the 2007 Regional New Voices contest.

I'm attaching the first ten pages of the novel, along with an SASE for your reply. Thanks so much for your consideration. I look forward to hearing from you.

Sincerely,
Future Lit Star

61 DO YOUR HOMEWORK

An Interview with Cosmic Editor

Cosmic Editor, the warmhearted and tattooed veteran of two major publishing houses, has a decade of experience acquiring and editing new fiction and nonfiction titles. You'll find Cosmic Editor's real name in the acknowledgments section of many of your favorite books.

ASIDE FROM A FABULOUS BOOK OR PROPOSAL, WHAT ARE THE BEST THINGS YOU CAN SEE IN A NEW AUTHOR'S COVER LETTER AND BIO IN TERMS OF RÉSUMÉ ITEMS?

For me, it's a bit more than a list of résumé items. Here are a few things that I find appealing:

- Previous publications, awards, affiliations, etc.
- If nonfiction, professional credentials, etc., that speak to the author's expertise on the project at hand. Professional credits are good for fiction, too, of course. Teaching creative writing, for example, shows you know something about craft.

- Knowledge of the particular publishing house's list or area of specialty. This goes for querying an agent, too—knowledge of the agent's list. Unfortunately, sometimes authors don't do their homework and as a result don't really know where they're sending their work. A little rooting around can go a long way, even if it's just referencing a particular book the house published that is similar to the author's, or just a book the author really liked. Generally this shows that the author has spent some time researching, which in turn shows a level of care and willingness to go the extra mile—good qualities in a prospective author.

- Some knowledge of the market that isn't dated. If I read one more time that *Books for Me 'n You* mag said in 1998 that rocket science is the fastest-growing market, I'm going to hurl. But noting that Alice Sebold's *Lucky Bones* was a surprise bestseller during a summer when missing teenage girls were making headlines and "my new book is a personal narrative of the summer my best friend disappeared," well, the dots are connected. (Perhaps this reference will be dated by pub date, but authors should stay informed. Where/when possible, subscribe to industry sites like publishersmarketplace.com—a great resource for anyone looking to both educate herself about the industry and see what's being sold and who's buying it.)

- Lack of bombast. This is tricky. You need to sell yourself, but to say "My book will sell a million copies in the first year" and "This is bigger than *Da Vinci*" just may induce eye-rolling rather than excitement.

- This isn't a résumé thing per se, but it is apropos: Much like a job interview, the cover letter is the author's sales pitch, it is the author's representative. You wouldn't go to an interview with stained, wrinkled clothes, unprepared, answering questions with "I don't know, but Donald

> Trump would love me and I would win *The Apprentice*." By the same token, it amazes me that some queries only reflect that the author is sloppy and hasn't really put a lot of time and effort into making the best impression. It may seem fussy to complain about typos in a cover letter, but misspelling the house's name doesn't instill a lot of confidence. This goes for letters querying agents as well as editors.

ANY MORE TIPS ON THE KIND OF QUERY YOU WANT TO SEE?

If authors are looking at *Literary Marketplace* or at agents' Web sites, or any of the other sources, they should absolutely follow the guidelines. If it says, "Send query via snail mail only," it's not wise to assume that you're going to get somewhere by e-mailing. Frankly, that's just another reason to delete. The sad truth is that, like everyone else, agents and editors are busy, and as much as we want to find the next book we can't turn down, there is such a high volume of material coming in that it's easier to find reasons to say no than to say yes. The author's job is to make it impossible for us to say no.

DO YOU CARE IF THE WRITER HAS AN M.F.A. IN CREATIVE WRITING OR A JOURNALISM DEGREE?

It's less about the degree itself than the connections that come with it: who will blurb or big-mouth the book, does that university have a history of supporting its published alumni, etc., as well as the quality of the program. The impact of the degree does to a certain extent depend on the project: If it's a novel and the author has a degree from the Iowa Writers' Workshop? Yes, since that's a hallmark of quality, I'll look twice. If the author went to Pinochle U. but studied with Cormac McCarthy? Sure, that will grab me. If the author went to either Iowa or P-U and won writing awards? That doesn't hurt.

At the end of the day, the university credentials don't make or break it, but they can help in the initial assessment.

IS THERE ANY POINT IN SUBMITTING A QUERY OR MANUSCRIPT DIRECTLY TO AN EDITOR AT A LARGE PUBLISHING HOUSE? AT A SMALL PUBLISHING HOUSE? OR SHOULD FOLKS FOCUS ON GETTING AN AGENT?

This is a good question, and you will hear all sorts of answers, from "Hell no, we won't even look at it" to "Suuuuuure . . . We'll get back to you in two years."

Seriously, I read everything—well, at least every query—that comes across my desk, but that's not necessarily a policy shared by other editors I know. The truth is that nobody really has the time to go through unsolicited stuff slowly and carefully. That said, I don't think queries hurt. The best thing authors can do to increase their chances of getting attention? Do their homework and send out an outstanding query. Authors should not send full manuscripts until asked, and authors should always include a SASE—yes, with return postage.

As for agent or not: Good agents are an author's advocate. They step in and handle things that an author may not feel comfortable doing—negotiating advance, asking questions about marketing and publicity, etc. Agents can play "bad cop" when you feel like asking a question that may somehow negatively impact your relationship with your house. The good ones do really earn their commission and can be worth their weight in gold. The problem with getting an agent is of course the same problem with querying a publishing house directly—some agents only want authors who have published before, etc. This is why following the Ariel Gore program will really help you out. You make yourself a lit star, and agents and editors are gonna notice, whether it's from your query, your blog, or your appearance at Nude Pie-Throwing Night at Oklahoma's Okiefest.

HOW DO YOU FEEL ABOUT SELF-PUBLISHED WRITING CREDITS? I'M GUESSING YOU AREN'T ESPECIALLY THRILLED TO HEAR THAT SOMEONE PUT OUT THEIR OWN ZINE OR PUT THEIR FIRST NOVEL OUT THROUGH A PRINT-ON-DEMAND OUTFIT, BUT YOU MIGHT BE INTERESTED IN THE AUDIENCE THEY DEVELOPED THROUGH THESE ENDEAVORS.

Exactly. Publishing is changing all the time. Places like iUniverse.com are helping people get their work into printed form. The important thing to keep in mind is that, obviously, books—whether self-pubbed or big-pubbed—do not sell themselves. If you embark on the self-publishing route, the most impressive thing you can do is make sure your book sells like hotcakes—that's what makes the bigger guys take note. As for zines, it's good information to know—most important would be any sort of distribution numbers or any "endorsements," any local/regional/national following you may have garnered, or any sort of recognition the work has received.

OKAY, SO NOW THE AUTHOR HAS SUFFICIENTLY WOOED YOU AND YOU REQUEST THE ACTUAL MANUSCRIPT—OR IT'S A NONFICTION BOOK AND YOU'VE BOUGHT IT ON PROPOSAL. WHAT ARE A FEW COMMON MISTAKES AUTHORS MAKE IN ACTUALLY EXECUTING A BOOK PROJECT? WHAT MAKES YOU GO, "DAMMIT! AND THEY WERE SO CHARMING. . . ."

Usually with fiction you know what you're getting—unless the author is known to the house or known to the world, a full manuscript is offered. If there are huge problems or questions about the manuscript, chances are the publisher/editor will ask for revisions before committing—that's if the changes are pretty extensive. With fiction, if I have any early editing thoughts, I always try to lay them out before making an offer. Both author and editor need to be up front if there's going to be resistance to changing a character's name or not having Aunt Mimi die in Chapter 78. Something that I would caution authors about is a certain amount of "preciousness." Yes, it's your baby and you know better than anyone else, etc., but the editor's expertise also needs to be trusted. I understand integrity of the word and story, but an ongoing argument over something that just ain't gonna fly isn't the best use of everyone's time.

Personally, I get irritated with laziness. Revision means re-vision. Revision means "Take a look at the whole and see how this material is going to be altered by addition or subtraction, and then tackle accordingly." Also, if I make comments about ways in which overall, say, Chapter 1 isn't working, the author should be able to apply that to subsequent chapters. None of this is to say that I, as an editor, assume the authors I work with are going to take all of my suggestions—hell, no. For me, the editing process is a dialogue, but it should be a respectful give-and-take.

CAN YOU OFFER ANY TIPS TO AUTHORS ON HOW TO BE EDITED?

How to be edited? Be up front with your editor about your expectations, your own hopes/questions about your project/manuscript, and any particular guidance you are looking for. You should expect that there are things—comments, suggestions, edits—you will simply not agree with, and with that in mind: Don't whine. Don't like a suggestion? Talk to your editor about it. Be respectful. Don't like a suggestion? Remember that it's coming from a place of knowledge. Trust your editor. And make sure your editor trusts you. This is pretty essential. Obviously there are some relationships that aren't meant to be, but since your editor is generally your first contact with a house and, after the publicity and marketing phase has ended, your long-term contact, a certain amount of trust is necessary.

ONCE THE BOOK IS EDITED AND PRIOR TO PUBLICATION, WHAT IS AN AUTHOR'S JOB? SIT TIGHT AND SPEAK WHEN SPOKEN TO? SEND IN A BUNCH OF COVER IDEAS? PLAN A TOUR WITHOUT DISCUSSING IT WITH YOU? I'LL ADMIT I HAVE A HARD TIME WITH THIS EVEN AFTER DOING SEVEN BOOKS. I WANT TO BE HELPFUL WITHOUT BEING HIGH-MAINTENANCE; I WANT TO HAVE SOME CONTROL OVER THE THINGS THAT ARE IMPORTANT TO ME, BUT ACCEPT THAT WHILE IT'S MY BOOK, IT'S THE PUBLISHER'S PRODUCT.

Authors should work to drum up as much action—publicity—as possible, but authors should also know that the best publicity is timed with publication. If it's too early, it won't help book sales. I appreciate an author who wants to work with the publisher, knowing the realities of the situation—that there are more and more books being published, giving publicists less and less time to devote to each book. Authors can't afford to just sit back and wait for things to happen. That said, an author should keep the publisher in the loop regarding anything she's planning, to make sure efforts aren't duplicated and that everything works out timing-wise. As with everything else, keep the lines of communication open. And be realistic. Of course everyone wants to be on *Oprah*. And of course not everyone can be on *Oprah*. The publisher has to choose its shots. While your book on snakes in seventeenth-century France is well-written and intriguing, it just may not be a natural for *Oprah*. Or *People* magazine. Asking your editor or publicist seventy-eight times to pitch *Oprah* isn't going to get you pitched to *Oprah*, but it may get you labeled a pain in the butt. As always, if you have major concerns or questions, don't sit on them until your book is on the shelves and you realize that you haven't told your publicist you can't bear to speak on the radio.

And it must be said: It's true, books are products. The publishing house wants the book to be a huge success as much as you do, but there are realities and limitations. Keep yourself informed, ask questions, and be prepared to become a self-publicizing machine. If you have an agent, remember that your agent is your advocate, and should you feel uncomfortable about asking anything, your agent can always check in on your behalf.

NONE OF MY STUDENTS BELIEVE ME WHEN I TELL THEM THEY DON'T GET TO CHOOSE THEIR OWN BOOK COVERS AND MAY NOT HAVE ANY INPUT WHATSOEVER. HOW MANY TIMES HAVE YOU USED A COVER SUPPLIED BY AN AUTHOR?

Sorry to break hearts. No, authors often don't get to choose their own covers. How often have I used a cover supplied by an author? Um, never?

That said, I always try to ask early on what the author is envisioning for the cover—I want to know right away what she is thinking because authors generally have very strong ideas about their covers. Heck, I have strong opinions about what "my" books should look like. The quandary comes when an author has one distinct idea and nothing else will do. Of course, from the author's perspective, it's also an issue when the publisher has one distinct idea and nothing else will do.

I would counsel all authors to simply be aware that they do not get to design their covers. They may have a lot of input, they may have very little, but there can be a lot of cooks in the kitchen—the art department, the editor, the publisher—and what will "win" is what everyone feels will really sell. It's really depressing when everyone in the house is convinced that they've knocked the cover outta the park, and the lone holdout is the author, who simply hates it. By the way, I recognize that all you lit stars in the making may be thinking, *Well, I'd be pretty depressed, too—IT'S MY BOOK.* As with anything else, keep the lines of communication open, and remember that the folks on the other side of the desk have been doing this for a while and they do have the best interests of the book in mind. There's no guarantee that your cover will be altered to suit your vision, but sharing your thoughts/concerns in a tactful, well-thought-out way rather than picking up the phone and yelling "I hate it!" may well increase your chances of being heard.

If there are real issues with the cover—if you feel that it misrepresents the book, will turn off the target audience, etc.—then the publishing house needs to know that.

I think some authors may have the idea that the design process is haphazard. They are so close to their book that they feel no one else can capture it. But there are a lot of things to consider—what's out there, what's worked, what hasn't, what is truly marketable. All of this sounds really negative, so I do have to say: I have seen plenty of covers that have been greeted with universal love. Those are great moments.

COSMIC EDITOR'S ASSIGNMENTS

the cocktail party exercise!

One of the things that your book needs is a hook. What is your book in two minutes / two sentences or less? If you can't narrow it down, that might be a sign that you gotta do some more work in figuring out what your book is, who it's for, and why the world needs it. It's called the Cocktail Party Exercise because it's the perfect two-minute conversation: "Oh, Mary, nice to meet you. You're a vegan chef specializing in fungus sculpture? Great. I'm working on a book called *The Surprise in the Kitchen*—it's *The Prize Winner of Defiance, Ohio* meets *Raw: The Uncook Book* and should really appeal to foodies and pop culture fanatics."

jacket copy

Another exercise for you fictioneers: Write your own jacket copy, meaning work on your synopsis. It's amazing how the most gifted writers turn into textbook bores when trying to craft an enticing synopsis. As with your cover letter and honing your cocktail party pitch, your synopsis should make your novel sound as enticing and compelling as it is. Rather than thinking of this as a chore, think of all the copy you read on book jackets when you're perusing the shelves in your local bookstore. What grabs you? What makes you stuff the book back, spine in? Remember, your goal is to make it impossible for an editor or agent to say no.

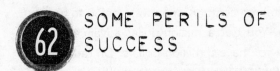

62 SOME PERILS OF SUCCESS

In the off-the-record after-banter of my interviews with some of the biggest lit stars—the ones who've found commercial success—I heard a common dread. The complaints were different, but the fear was constant:

"My advance was too big."

"I can't take this thing to the next level."

"The movie is stalled in development."

And "My book was only on the bestseller lists for five weeks. I'm going to lose my house."

Some of the made-it lit stars I visited, expecting to find them resting on down-stuffed laurel pillows, were nervous.

I know what you're thinking. *A too-big advance?! That's their problem?* But on scales large and small, this is real.

What is an advance, anyway? It's a sum of money the publisher gives you in advance of your book actually earning any royalties. Your publisher is making a bet that your book will sell X number of copies and is fronting you the money you'll earn. Let's say your book is going to sell for ten dollars and you're going to get 10 percent in royalties. That's a buck a book. Your publisher gives you a $20,000 advance and let's say your book sells fifteen thousand copies. That's great. It didn't quite hit the mark and you'll never see another dime in royalties, but everybody's pleased. Now let's say you sold that same book to a much more gung-ho publisher who was sure that historical novels set in fifteenth-century Japan were going to be the next big thing. You got a million-dollar advance. That's excellent. Now you have a million dollars. Or, rather, you have about $400,000 after your agent, the IRS, and your ex-wife found out about it. Still, you've got close to half a million bucks and you're feeling pretty special. The publisher, having invested all this cash, is going to pull out all the stops for publicity and marketing. Your face on billboards. Fifty cities in forty days and an international satellite-radio tour. You're hobnobbing with all the big-time reviewers. You get pedicures and buy a new house (if you're smart, you pay cash for it—don't ever rely on sales figures to pay a mortgage, and don't ever count your royalties before the check clears the bank).

So, everything's going swimmingly until . . . your book sells fifteen thousand copies. Suddenly your publisher on the phone sounds like some irate father: "I paid for you to go to Princeton and you want to be a waiter?!" What would make most parents proud ("My son has a job!") can make Princeton parents rather grumpy. So now Big Daddy's frowning big time in the form of your sales report. Anytime you get an advance for a book, until you sell through that advance, your sales report will actually express your earnings as a negative number. This can be kind of depressing. A little quarterly note reminding you just how much money your publisher has lost on you. Now, before you have a panic attack, you're not going to have to pay that money back to the publisher or anything. Still, your masterpiece historical novel is being remaindered, returned, recycled. And you're feeling like a major, major loser.

It's something successful people don't talk about publicly because they know it sounds whiny and ungrateful. Not only that, but they don't want to tell anyone their blockbuster only sold fifteen thousand copies. They know it's a problem thousands of unpublished writers only wish they had. Part of their torment is that they're supposed to be good Americans and go around saying they feel "blessed" all the time. And they do feel blessed. It's just that they feel this other thing, too. This dread. Success is relative. And there's always a shinier lit star. You got booked on *Good Morning America* and the publisher printed fifty thousand copies? Great. But now 50 percent of them have been returned. What now? Selling twenty-five thousand copies of a book is respectable by anybody's standards (most books sell less than a thousand copies). At a small press you might have gotten a permanent poster, signed and smiling, in the entryway. At a big press where they expected much more, the subtext of your next e-mail from your editor might sound a lot like "Your career is in the toilet."

I got a $100,000 advance for my first book. A welfare cutoff notice on my door and a phone call from my agent promising more money than I'd ever heard of. We're talking rags to riches. "And then this guy showed up with a glass slipper. . . ." This was 1996—the days of Internet bubbles and Gen X gravy book deals—but we didn't know it at the time. Children of divorce, all, but we still believed in happily ever after.

My book did very well, but it did not sell a hundred thousand copies. For a constellation of reasons, including sales figures, the placement of Saturn in my astrological chart, my editor's decision to quit and move to Georgia, and my failure to act on several cryptic directives from the new editor, my next deal got canceled. I could have called it a day, of course. Rejection bites. Instead, I e-mailed the other authors I knew until two suggested the same editor at the same small feminist press in Seattle. I gave that editor a call and sent her my manuscript. I didn't want a big advance, I told her. I wanted to deal in reality. For five years and five books, I stuck with Seal Press. And we dealt in reality. In those five years, the small feminist press in

Seattle became part of a larger press in the Bay Area and New York. And I sold a lot of books. I didn't get huge advances. I didn't get huge publicity budgets. But I got a lot of freedom—editorial freedom and the freedom to organize my own tours, complete with shadow puppet shows and singing divas. If one of my books sold twenty-five thousand copies out the door and hit a national best-seller list, that was great. If another sold five thousand copies, that was "nothing to sneeze at," my editor assured me. But Seal Press hardly ever publishes fiction, so when I wrote my first novel, it was time to find a new publisher. My agent shopped the manuscript around and sold the book to HarperSanFrancisco, a press that seemed like the best of all worlds—a small, attentive staff in San Francisco backed by the publicity and marketing muscle of HarperCollins in New York. Someday I'll know the numbers—first printing, cartons orders, books returned, royalty-earning copies sold—but I don't *want* to know the numbers. I wrote the best book I could, will do my monkey-suit best to promote it, and the numbers will be the numbers. I want to write my next book.

One successful author told me he was just waiting to get to the "fuck-you stage."

"Meaning?"

"Meaning that neither my ego nor my finances are dependent on my sales figures. Then I'll be able to do whatever I want."

Oh, that stage. Ever-elusive. As a rising lit star, you'd be wise to make sure your survival-finances are never dependent on your sales figures. And except to the extent that your ego can help you by fueling you with competitive energy, you'd be wise to let your ego depend on something else, too. Make sure you always have the freedom to say "Fuck you."

Literary careers don't just rise and rise and rise. The publishing business is fickle, unpredictable. Just because your last book won the Pulitzer doesn't mean anyone will buy your next book. Hell, they might not even buy the prizewinner. The trajectory of your publishing experience might not go from self-publishing your first book to finding a small press for your second to cashing in big on your third and fourth and fifth.

This is a creative life you're building, after all, not a fairy tale you're living out.

So, when you hit it big in the publishing business, take a word of wisdom from the old masters. In the hexagram called "Abundance," the I-Ching says, "Clarity within, movement without. The king attains abundance. Be not sad. Be like the sun at midday. Such a time of abundance is usually brief. Therefore a sage might well feel sad in view of the decline that must follow. But such sadness does not befit him. He must be like the sun at midday, illuminating and gladdening everything under heaven."

Geddit?

63 ASK MAGNIFICENT METEOR

Rising Lit Star asks: How important is good writing versus good selling? I see plenty of okay-but-not-great writing placed in decent-paying markets. How'd they do that?

Magnificent Meteor reveals: They did that by producing good, consistent writing, by pushing it with good selling, and by always delivering usable work on deadline. An editor would rather work with a pretty good writer who's going to deliver than a great writer who might come through. You don't want to get in the habit of producing and publishing mediocre work—sometimes writers get lazy after they've developed relationships with steady markets—but don't be afraid to lower your standards at eleven P.M. on the night of your midnight deadline. Done and acceptable is always better than not done and brilliant. Or maybe they slept with the editor.

Rising Lit Star asks: How do I get someone interested in my sorta run-on-sentence, life-story memoir that is basically my version of *A Million Little Pieces* and *Running with Scissors?*

Magnificent Meteor reveals: Once your manuscript is roughly the way you want it—and preferably you have some writing credits for shorter pieces at this point—it's time to prepare a query. A query is a short letter (see "Get an Agent") and the first ten pages of your book. It's great that you have other books to compare it to—those comparisons will help an agent or editor get a quick take on the book. Mention those in your letter. Find the agents who sold those books. Query them about yours. If you're interested in any smaller presses, check their Web sites for submissions guidelines, read a few of the books they've published, and submit.

Rising Lit Star asks: How would you recommend getting the attention of well-to-do publishers?

Magnificent Meteor reveals: Start small. Publish everywhere. Contribute to everything. Get your name out there. You will get attention.

Rising Lit Star asks: Do you need an agent? How do you get one? What do they really do for you? How do you make yourself attractive to one? How do you know if they're good?

Magnificent Meteor reveals: Agents are the middlemen between authors and publishers. They get acquisition editors excited about your book, negotiate your deal, actually read your contract and cross out the obnoxious bits, and take 15 percent of your money.

You need an agent if you want to sell a book to a midsized or big press. An agent makes money on commission, so you don't pay them up front. This means the agent needs you as much as you need her. You get an agent by asking your writer acquaintances for references, by consistently putting yourself out there as a writer or "expert" in your field until you hear of an appropriate agent, or by looking in the acknowledgments section of books you like and then finding the agent's Web site. Check out the submissions guidelines and read a few of the books they've successfully sold so you can write a cover letter that makes it clear you've done your homework.

Rising Lit Star asks: What are the points at which your integrity is more important than your paycheck—particularly in a prepublication working life? How do you know when to just jump off the cliff, or when to wait for a safety net?

Magnificent Meteor reveals: This is probably applicable to your postpublication working life, too, since publication doesn't pay that much. Your reasonable rent or mortgage is more important than your integrity. Just because you're an artiste doesn't mean you can be a freeloader—unless you are very, very cute. If you have kids, feeding them is more important than your integrity. After that, jump off the cliff! No need to worry about feeding or clothing yourself or always having the electricity on or student loans or your credit rating or anything else.

Rising Lit Star asks: I have a piece that I'm sure a big zine in L.A. would accept because it fits in perfectly with their upcoming issue. However, I was thinking that I should work on it a bit more and submit it to a bigger review in the hopes that I might get a little more exposure. On the one hand, I think I should just get it out there. On the other, I don't want to publish something that might not get published elsewhere because it's "already been published."

Magnificent Meteor reveals: Good question. For nonfiction, I'd say just get it out there wherever you can and then rewrite it as a new article for the larger publication. This way you can tell the big boys, "I've written on this same topic of sewer management for Big L.A. Zine." Nonfiction writers are constantly repackaging the same story for republication—they call it an "area of expertise." I call it recycling. But there's nothing wrong with recycling.

PART FIVE

become a brazen self-promoter

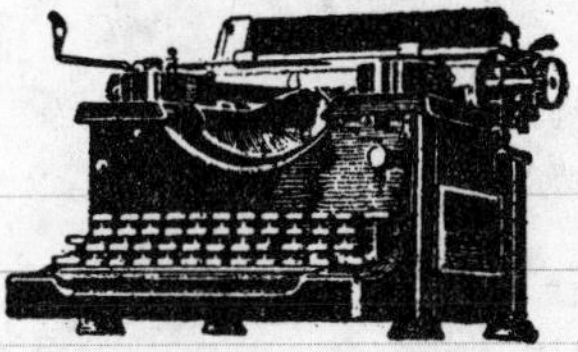

Good things happen to those who hustle.

—Anaïs Nin

64 LEARN TO TALK

Anaïs Nin didn't learn to speak until she was thirty. Maya Angelou went through a mute period only to become one of the most eloquent people on the planet. I'm no Anaïs Nin or Maya Angelou, but lemme tell ya, if I can get through a reading, you can, too.

Some people come to writing through a love of reading. I came to writing primarily because I could not talk. Owl child, they called me. Wide-eyed and mute. Even in college, I did not speak. When asked to read a paper aloud, I stuttered excuses and began to shake. I'd spent my adolescence in Asia and Europe, where introverts are still allowed, but I was in America now. As my secret ambition spouted and flowered, I had to face facts: In America, the recluse is an endangered species. In no other country is shyness interpreted as arrogance, and in no other language I know does the same word mean both quiet and stupid. But here we are. It took me three years to teach myself to talk. At my first public reading, I looked out over the audience and, because everyone looked so eager, I ran. At my second, I stood behind the podium, looked down at my story, and let the words unjumble themselves on the page. I was ready. But even a thirty-second silence makes Americans nervous. "Next!" someone yelled from the crowd.

I sent out press releases, got myself booked on the radio. On a show on WGN, the host asked me what I'd studied in college. "Communications," I told him.

"Lotta good *that* did you," he chuckled.

After those first awkward interviews, I'd lie awake in bed, replaying in my mind every ridiculous thing I'd said. In the dark, I thought of brilliant answers and imagined how the interview might have gone, *if only* . . . But I kept putting myself out there. Painfully. Again and again. And, you know, a funny thing happens when you practice. I'll probably never change my core. I don't want to. Meet me at a party and you'll likely notice my awkward and halting conversation, but give me a mic and I will perform. Throw impossible questions at me and I'll blurt out the answers. I've learned that no one really cares if you say something ridiculous, but no one will read your work if you don't tell them to. Maybe you can go back to being a hermit after you've got a few cult classics under your studded belt. In the meantime, you've got to play at being an extrovert. You've got to dazzle the three strangers who show up at your reading. You've got to send bold press releases to small-town zines and big-city newspapers. You've got to take to the radio waves. You've got to get on the phone and book yourself a tour. You've got to dress up like a circus monkey to get any attention around here. And when folks drive across town, generous-hearted, and show up to stare at you in your whacked outfit, you've got to perform. You're a lit star, dammit. And this is how you will rise. Open your mouth and force the words out. Again and again. Practice. And then practice some more. You don't have to be Anaïs Nin or Maya Angelou, but you've got to be able to get through a reading.

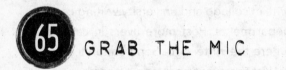

65 GRAB THE MIC

> It usually takes me more than three weeks to prepare a good impromptu speech.
>
> —**Mark Twain**

To learn how to do a reading—something you'll be all but forced to do when you publish a book—you just have to start doing it. And the sooner the better.

Check out your local weekly papers for spoken-word open mics in your town. Ask at your local independent bookstore. Check the bulletin board at the library. If you can't find anything going on . . . organize your own gig.

Readings are more fun when you have a little group of lit stars, so either get a few friends together or plan to make it an open mic. Plan it a couple of months in advance so you have time to pull it all together. Give the thing a snazzy title. Consider a flexible theme. See if you can find an established local writer or slam poet who'll agree to perform first.

You'll need a venue, so approach the managers at your favorite bookstore, café, gallery, or bar. You might be surprised at how easy it can be to get a business owner to give you a weekday evening spot if you've got a reasonable proposal. If you have any trouble, check listings at the Web site letsdoitontheroad.com for spoken-word-friendly venues.

Once you've got your venue, start publicizing your event. Post flyers in college and university writing centers and English departments. Post more flyers in cafés and libraries. Go where the writers go. Send announcements to local papers. List the event on Internet boards.

Decide on some ground rules before your event, such as . . . a *time limit* for each reader. Most audiences can't handle more than about an hour of readings, so count the number of writers you've got and divvy the hour up.

At home before the event, practice the stories or poems you want to read. Time yourself. Practice in front of the mirror if that makes you feel better. Practice in the car. Don't mind the drivers in the other lanes who look at you like you're crazy talking to the dashboard. Put a cell phone to your ear and practice as you walk down the street. Get comfortable with your story. Try singing karaoke to get used to a crowd. A drunken crowd is easier to please than a room filled with people who might remember your name.

On the day of your event, call all of your friends and remind them to come. Resist the urge to start drinking at noon. Arrive at your venue early. And have fun!

66 "I STILL SHAKE ONSTAGE"

An Interview with Daphne Gottlieb

"Courage, by definition, doesn't mean not being afraid," says Daphne Gottlieb. "It means facing the things that scare you. Performing terrifies me."

Through the fear, she's anchored three national poetry tours, performed at festivals coast to coast, and toured with Slam America and Sister Spit. Of life on the road, she's said, "The best thing is always the unexpected generosity and kindness of strangers—the sudden intimacies of kinship where it's not foreseen—and the sporadic joy of driving along the highway to something too loud, driving too fast, while the rest of the world goes to its day jobs."

Her poetry, at once classical old-school and feminist gutter punk, has been praised as fierce, unapologetic, scorching, and deliriously gutsy.

Her book *Final Girl* was named one of the *Village Voice*'s Favorite Books of 2003, and *Why Things Burn* won a 2001 Firecracker Alternative Book Award and was a finalist for the Lambda Literary Award. She's the poetry editor of *Other Magazine* and several anthologies, including *Homewrecker: An Adultery Reader.*

HOW DO YOU SUGGEST A BEGINNER GET STARTED IN PUBLISHING AND PERFORMING?

Do the best writing you can, first and foremost. Make your work the best it can be. Then start searching out places that publish work like yours—there are a lot of online publications that have good readerships and aren't limited by the page constraints that print publications have, so the odds of getting published are better. Start going out to open mics and readings—find which ones you like, which ones feel nurturing. Start sharing when you feel comfortable. Don't feel like you have to read the first time you go somewhere. Listen and get a sense of the place. Practice your piece before you go, if it's your first time. Remember to breathe. Go more slowly than you think you should. Make sure your reading reflects the sense of the piece and you're not caught up in a canned poetry voice. Enjoy yourself.

DO YOU SEE YOURSELF AS A BORN PERFORMER, OR DID YOU LEARN HOW TO PERFORM YOUR POETRY IN ORDER TO COMMUNICATE IT TO THE WORLD?

I actually have terrible stage fright, though I have a background in theater. I think that shortly after I moved to San Francisco, I saw a bunch of young queers at Red Dora's—and later at Luna Sea—reading their work, and I felt this great sense of recognition—like, Wait! I can do that! And so I started approaching the organizers for spots in their shows. Out of that, the rest came.

CAN YOU ELABORATE ON THE REST?

It seemed like every time I performed, there was an organizer for another show in the audience—this was a really exciting time in San Francisco, with a lot of open mics and readings and shows—so I was lucky enough to get spots on bills. And I kept writing, and was lucky enough and worked hard enough to have a book. I'd started slamming at this point. I won a queer slam—my first. It wasn't as hard to win then as it is now, since it wasn't as well known. The win landed me a spot in the San Francisco semifinals. I went down like a glass jaw, but I was hooked. In 1998 I went to the National Poetry Slam, which was great timing, since I had a book coming out in 1999, so I was able to book a tour around these contacts. Since then, I've toured nationally three times or so and have been able to perform at some fairly large festivals.

WHAT'S YOUR DEFINITION OF SUCCESS?

That's kind of a tough question—it really changes from moment to moment and objective to objective. I think that, in a broad sense, achieving what I set out to do is how I define success, whether it's my intent with a particular poem, or editing an anthology, or reading a piece out loud. I think for poets, defining "success" is sort of a game of "Are we there yet?," since poetry will likely never pay our bills. So the measure of success has to come from somewhere else, somewhere inside.

THESE DAYS, HOW OFTEN DO YOU DO READINGS? DO YOU STILL FEEL STAGE FRIGHT?

It's hard to say how often I do readings—probably once or twice a month. It's a mix of stuff—sometimes it's a benefit, sometimes it's a reading series or a launch reading for another author. My stage fright is still awful, and I have no surefire technique for beating it. I still shake onstage. I try to remember to breathe and be aware of my feet. Mostly, I try to remember something someone once told me—that there's one person in that room who really needs to hear what I have to say. I didn't believe this for a long time, and still think it's pretty hokey, but over time, I've found that it seems to actually be the case. If I believe in what I'm saying, the conviction carries me through. If I don't believe in what I'm saying, I really don't have any business being up there in the first place.

DAPHNE'S ASSIGNMENT

your lineage

Make a list of three to five writers whose work has inspired you—maybe they're not your favorite writers, but they do something that you do in your work. Find out who inspired them and who their influences were. Read some of the writers who were formative for them. Discover your own writerly lineage—sometimes the influence of a writer will come through you, through your writing, before you've even read their work. Going back to the source can enrich your writing. Repeat as often as desired.

67 ALERT THE PRESS

Now that you've got a reading or an open mic or a book or a zine or a tour to promote to the world, you're going to need some press attention. You can buy ads in appropriate magazines and newspapers—especially if you've got a real niche audience and you know what periodicals they're reading—but who can afford more than a couple of ads? If you've got a zine, you can offer to trade ads with other zines, but what you really want is for the media to get your message out to their audiences without your having to pay for it. You want feature stories about you in your local papers, you want interviews in major and minor national magazines, you want reviews on the radio, you want to sit down with Robin Roberts on *Good Morning America*. And so you begin with a press release. Maybe even a whole press kit.

Now, when you send out a press release, you're asking a journalist to do you a favor. You want him to promote your zine, review your book, or announce your event. But most journalists don't have time to do you a favor. What you need to do is figure out what that journalist needs and hand it to him. What does a journalist need? you ask. He needs money, but he's not allowed to accept a bribe. What else does he need? He needs *stories*. A journalist is a storyteller just like you. If he ends up selling copies of your book or advertising your event while he's telling a good story, he doesn't mind, but his job is to find good stories and tell them. Your job, then, is to give him a true and relevant story. True is easy. Yes, you are bad-ass and, yes, you've written this book. What makes a story relevant is a little bit trickier. Is there some way the topic of your book can be connected to a current event—a news item, a trend, or a holiday? A nonfiction book on flirting might be a good story as Valentine's Day approaches. It's not necessary to make your story timely, but it sure helps. A novel about an outbreak of infectious disease in America might do very well when international epidemics are making headlines. Maybe you're bristling right now. *Take advantage of world tragedy*? But you have to understand: The publicity machine is a twisted game. And, truly, you are not taking advantage of world tragedy. You've written something true and important, have you not? If folks read it, the world will change. What do you care if the means of publicity feel inauthentic? What do you care if an ad for mattresses follows your media debut? All that's important is that *you* maintain your authenticity.

You'll notice a strange thing: Even in worlds like national television where it seems as if shallowness reigns supreme, a genuine soul can prevail. Even broadcast journalists are, above all, our fellow humans. If you have an important story to tell, that human might like nothing more than to help you tell it. Sure, there are bosses and advertisers, and you'll end up on the broadcaster's shit list if you tell her you're going to talk about your battle with brain cancer and then show up and start screaming about the military-industrial complex. But if you can honor the parameters mainstream journalists are working within, they just might return the favor and tell the world about your brand-new book. And then there's the story of *you.* Maybe you wrote a Southern romance while you were on a two-year tour in Iraq, jotting notes on scraps when you weren't being attacked by insurgents and risking life and limb. That's a good story. It might not have anything to do with the plot of your romance book, but it's a damn good story, and if it's true, you'll get in the paper with it.

If you have any lead time—maybe you're still working on your project and now just vaguely thinking about how you'll promote it in a year or two—it's excellent training to take a short internship at a small media outlet where the editors will let you read through all the press releases that pile up. Within a week or two, you'll begin to see the kind of story that catches your eye, the kind of thing you can easily turn around and pitch to your editor. If you don't have that kind of lead time, fear not. *I* had such an internship. And for the last twelve years I've been reading the press releases folks send to my zine.

Here's what I've observed:

- Ninety percent of the press releases that land in my post-office box are simply announcements. This book has been published and Armistead Maupin says it's brilliant. This zine is new and here's the zine. This reading is taking place at seven P.M. on Thursday, and even if you cared, I haven't given you enough time to publicize it. I glance over these press releases, think, *Oh, that's interesting,* and then I throw them away. If I had time, maybe I could report the story, interview the author, find the lead—the timeliness or the sexiness or the universal human-interest angle—and then I could write a feature story or a review. But I don't have time. Your press release has been recycled.

- The other 10 percent of press releases that find their way to my desk, I might actually be able to use. These are feature stories I can expand or print as is. I don't have to call you to find out you wrote the book while being showered with bullets and Molotov cocktails. It's all right here in the press release, and if I'm lucky, there's a photo to go with it. Maybe I'll do a short follow-up interview. If I'm super-intrigued, I might set up a time to come talk to you, re-report the story, take my own pictures. But if I'm on deadline and I've got a blank page, all I have to do is some quick fact-checking and I can print your press release practically verbatim. It may not be great journalism, but it's what often happens on deadline.

Here's my ideal press kit:

- A one-page press release (standard margins, normal font, and twelve- to fourteen-point type) that reads like a feature story (any angle that makes the story timely, maybe some background on why you wrote the book or made the zine, something about you that makes the whole thing fairytale-like, plus a quote or two from an "expert" or a reader).

- An active photo—color or black-and-white. A head shot is all right. It might work. But it's best if the picture shows the author in his element—slamming poetry or leading a workshop or fighting the war or doing something related to the subject of the book. If you can't afford to send a good print, it's all right if the press-release page includes a photo that's simply been scanned and photocopied. Under the image it should say: "Camera-ready photo available on request." This means that if I'm interested in the story you'll send me a print or e-mail me a scan in whatever format I need it.

- A one-page interview with *you*. This is a simple Q&A—questions you'd want the journalist to ask you if indeed he had time to call you. It should work as a sidebar to your press-release story or as a simple reference sheet where the journalist can get more information on the book or the zine or the event, catch a glimpse of your fabulous personality, and learn something about the circumstances that brought you to create this amazing project.

- A copy of the book or zine in question. Maybe the journalist will read it. More likely, he'll skim it and scan the cover to run with the article you've provided.

With these four elements, you make the journalist's job so easy, he has no real excuse to say no. If I'm the intern at the local weekly, I can turn around to my editor and say, "Hey, I've got a guy who wrote a romance novel while under siege in Iraq." At *Hip Mama,* I can take one look at your press kit and say, "Wow, this mother of toddlers found the time to self-publish her poetry chapbook. Great. And I happen to have a blank page." I plug it in and a few weeks later ten thousand mamas know what an inspiring thing you've done and where they can get a copy.

68 WHEN JOURNALISTS ARE NOT YOUR FRIENDS

Death will be a great relief. No more interviews.

—**Katharine Hepburn**

Most journalists are thoughtful and good-natured people who want to tell good stories and don't mind promoting your career while they're at it. But, alas, every profession has its bad apples, and journalism is no exception. Some journalists are frustrated novelists and zinesters who would like nothing more than to ridicule your novel or zine because they wish they'd written it themselves. Some journalists are not very bright and they think it makes them seem brighter when they make snide remarks in print about your genuine effort. Some journalists will ask you fair but tough questions about your intentions and your work and, if you look flustered, go in for the kill. And some journalists, while they may be perfectly well-adjusted and intelligent, just aren't going to *get* you. I've met all kinds. And being a basically trusting and naive fool, I usually reach for whatever toxic carrot they dangle. No press is bad press, they say, but some press is personally humiliating and professionally damaging. Some press sucks. I've been in tears for three days over a mean-spirited profile a two-bit reporter spewed about my life. The worst part is that it took me two and a half days to figure out why on earth I was so upset. Logically and realistically I can say, "Who cares?" But public scorn hurts.

For an owl child who's trying really hard to be a public grown-up, it's more painful than a physical attack. Worse than the ridicule is the sense of betrayal. This is business, but when we're talking about our creative work and our life histories, it sure feels personal. And this journalist *didn't* ask me hard questions. She was from where I'm from. She posed as friend and ally. She praised me and she praised my book. She asked bizarre questions and spun the conversation out until I made a few idiotic-sounding remarks and *ting! There she had it!* She didn't have to include her half of the conversation—she just took a few dumb-ass quotes out of context, called me incoherent, and suggested that I was on drugs. This kind of thing is the only part of the business that truly makes me want to quit. Maybe it's a kind of arrogance on my part, a case of taking myself too seriously. Even so, it really does makes me want to crawl into a cave and write my little books and not let anyone read them until I'm dead. But interviews-gone-bad come with the territory. And I have no great advice for you when it comes to surviving them except to say that if they make you feel as worthless and heartbroken as they make me feel, you're not alone. All together now, let's repeat after Katharine Hepburn: "I don't care what is written about me so long as it isn't true."

69 THE QUEEN OF SELF-PROMOTION

An Interview with Margaret Cho

Margaret Cho grew up in 1970s San Francisco surrounded by "old hippies, ex-druggies, burnouts from the sixties, drag queens, and Chinese people." Naturally, she started performing stand-up as a teenager.

In the early 1990s, she won a comedy contest where first prize was opening for Jerry Seinfeld. She moved to Los Angeles, hit the college circuit, and soon became the most-booked act in the market. Arsenio Hall introduced her to late night, Bob Hope put her on a prime-time special, and in 1994 she starred in the short-lived ABC sitcom *All-American Girl.* Hollywood producers watered down Margaret's script, told her she was too fat to play herself, and basically fucked with her self-esteem until any lesser woman would have crawled back to San Francisco to become a nameless fag hag. Not Margaret. She chronicled the whole debacle in a brilliant off-Broadway one-woman show called *I'm The One That I Want.* She toured the country, put out a best-selling book, and became a superstar on her own terms. With one independent success under her belt, she launched *Notorious C.H.O.* in 2001, a smash-hit thirty-seven-city national tour that culminated in a sold-out show at Carnegie Hall. Two years later, she set off on her third sold-out national tour, *Revolution,* and in 2003 she took her politically charged *State of Emergency* tour through the swing states of the presidential election.

Lauded as "murderously funny!" by the *New York Times*, *State of Emergency* eventually evolved into her fourth national show, *Assassin*, her most political work to date. Her second book, *I Have Chosen to Stay and Fight*, is pure righteous comic rage.

As if her insanely busy touring schedule isn't enough, she writes an award-winning blog at margaretcho.com, and has taken up belly dancing. For promoting equal rights wherever she goes, she's been honored by more civil rights organizations than you can shake a stick at. "I didn't mean to be a role model," she says. "I just speak my truth. I guess speaking from your heart really creates a huge impact, and if I can encourage people to do that, then I would love to be a role model. If I could encourage people to use their voices loudly, then that's my reward. I don't care about winning an Academy Award; I don't care about mainstream acceptance, because it's never going to be what I want it to be. I just want to do my work and love it."

HOW DID YOU KEEP FOCUSED ON YOUR TALENTS AFTER THE SITCOM EXPERIENCE? IT SEEMS THAT YOU HAD THIS ALLEGED "GREAT" OPPORTUNITY TO BE ON A SITCOM, WHICH I AM SURE WAS VERY EXCITING, TO HAVING YOUR SELF-ESTEEM ATTACKED IN REALLY NASTY WAYS. YOU TALK A LOT ABOUT THIS IN *I'M THE ONE THAT I WANT*, BUT HOW DID YOU COME TO WRITE THAT SHOW? WHAT DID YOU GO THROUGH IN YOUR HEART?

I wasn't thinking about much else. I was so obsessed with my own failure that I had to put my frustration somewhere. Doing a show about it was the best thing I could have done because it answered all the questions people had about it and it helped me feel better. I think writing is best when it feels uncontrollable—when you have to write about something because it is burning you up inside or you have nothing else you want to talk about but that one thing, it always comes out great.

A LOT OF PEOPLE THINK OF MADONNA AS THE QUEEN OF SELF-PROMOTION. TO ME, YOU ARE THE QUEEN OF SELF-PROMOTION. WILL YOU SHARE SOME OF YOUR STRATEGIES?

I don't know why Madonna would be considered the Queen of Self-Promotion, because she has always had huge corporate sponsorship. She has had major play on all the media outlets. She gets every magazine cover. All her efforts are supported by the mainstream, who actually do her promotion! All she does is produce work, which can be controversial and incendiary, but as far as publicity goes, she has always had lots of help.

I have to promote myself entirely, which doesn't mean to say that I don't get help from the media outlets, but I really have to work to get whatever I can. I am not welcomed by the mainstream, so I have to seek other outlets. I produce my own films, I am always writing, always trying to think of things, what can I do to get the word out—anything!

PEOPLE ARE ALWAYS TELLING ME THAT I AM "BRAVE" FOR WRITING SUCH DEEPLY PERSONAL THINGS. WHILE I UNDERSTAND WHY FOLKS MIGHT THINK THIS, IT IS NOT MY EXPERIENCE. I DO NOT FEEL "BRAVE." I FEEL LIKE I AM

PLAYING THE HAND I'VE BEEN DEALT. I IMAGINE THAT A LOT OF PEOPLE DESCRIBE YOU AS BEING "BRAVE," AND I AM WONDERING IF YOU ALSO FIND THIS A TAD BAFFLING. IF SO, WILL YOU DEFINE *BRAVERY*?

I don't know if what I do is brave, and bravery has lots of different meanings for people. I think bravery is standing up for what you believe in, in the face of extreme opposition, but most people I know have to do that because they cannot live any other way. So brave is just kind of normal.

DOES IT FEEL ANY DIFFERENT TO WRITE FOR READERS THAN TO WRITE FOR LISTENERS? WHAT INSPIRED YOU TO SIT DOWN AND WRITE A BOOK?

It isn't so different. I just write, and it is for everybody and everything. . . . I didn't really get inspired to write a book. I just had a lot of writing that had accumulated over time on my Web site that seemed right for a book. Right now in my life, I don't know if I could actually think about writing a book. It seems like such a daunting thing. Books are part of the entitled, privileged world that I don't feel a part of, so I could never approach it like that.

DO YOU HAVE A THEME SONG?

I am kind of obsessed with the song "Wichita Lineman." It's been covered by lots of people, and my favorite is Glen Campbell. It makes me wish that I lived on a mountain and drank coffee brewed with chicory.

MARGARET'S ASSIGNMENT

passions

I think the best thing to do is make a list of things that you love. That is very inspiring, and very interesting because you can really see who the person is, because there is passion there. If I get stuck, I write about things I love, like my dogs, or belly dancing, or tattoos, and it usually leads me somewhere else, a place I wouldn't have gone if I hadn't been writing passionately.

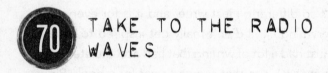

70 TAKE TO THE RADIO WAVES

The good old-fashioned radio: an elegant and effective place to promote your work. You can send standard press releases to community and national stations and they might very well call you to set up an interview. I've got a better idea: Become a self-styled expert in the field of your choosing. NPR can only review my book once, but they can call me back again and again to ask my opinion on anything from changes in maternity-leave laws to the young feminist trend toward reinventing the sex industry to why Marc Acito is so damn cute. And every time I show up, they'll promote something I do. If I'm talking abut family law, they'll call me "Ariel Gore, author of *The Hip Mama Survival Guide*." If I'm talking about the pros and cons of taking a year off to see the world before starting college, they'll call me "Ariel Gore, author of the vagabond memoir *Atlas of the Human Heart.*" If I'm talking about the rise and fall and rise again of the zine revolution, they'll call me "Ariel Gore, editor/publisher of *Hip Mama.*" And if I'm talking about the political tension between religious literalists and religious mystics, they'll call me "Ariel Gore, author of *The Traveling Death and Resurrection Show.*"

What are you an expert in? What can you *make* yourself an expert in? Anything in your personal or professional life can become "expert" material. Anything you've written about, researched, lived, or earned a degree in. Every time something related to your expertise starts making headlines, send quick press releases to local and national broadcast media. These journalists need you and they need your point of view. You won't get paid, but they'll mention your name and they'll mention your product. Just don't ever say "fuck" on the radio. They don't like that.

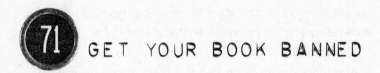

71 GET YOUR BOOK BANNED

To oppose something is to maintain it.

—**Ursula K. Le Guin**

In April of 2000, the Chinese government banned Wei Hui's debut novel, *Shanghai Baby,* for its "worship of Western culture" and graphic female-centered sex scenes. The young author was denounced as decadent and debauched, forty thousand copies of her book were publicly burned, her editor was fired, and—predictably—*Shanghai Baby* became an international bestseller.

In our heart of hearts, we all want to be loved and accepted. As authors, we want good reviews, positive attention. *If they don't have something nice to say, why do they say anything at all?* But youth culture, openness about sexuality, and revolutionary ideas are always met with resistance. And sometimes it's the folks we piss off with our writing who end up being the most helpful when it comes to getting our work out to a larger audience.

Once, when I praised single and teen moms on a public radio show in New York, so many listeners called in rage at me—one even saying that she thought my kid should be taken away and put in an orphanage because I wasn't married—I felt totally defeated. I slumped at my desk, buried my face in my hands. I felt like such a loser. I mean, I already felt pretty funky about not being able to feed my kid anything but lentils and rice—did they really have to rub it in? Maybe she *would* be better off in an orphanage. I hated those listeners, but I wondered if they were right.

Brring, brring. "Hello?"

And who should it be but a literary agent from New York. "I heard you on the radio," she said. "You're very controversial."

"Huh?"

"Do you have a book proposal?"

"Yes," I lied, brightening up. "It's just about ready. I'll have it on your desk in two weeks."

And of course I did have it on her desk in two weeks.

Those mean and angry listeners who meant to hurt my spirit turned out to be my literary angels. Their anger made me come across as "edgy." Controversy is a good thing.

You don't want to waste your time thinking up scandalous things to say just for shock value—that's silly—but never let your fear of conflict or disapproval keep you from telling your truth.

As a writer, part of your job is to make people uncomfortable, to push the envelope, to expose what's really going on in the world, to challenge, to tell the truth. If you succeed, you might get raged at on the radio. You might get called decadent and debauched. If you succeed, your books might get challenged, panned in reviews, banned in libraries, even destroyed. But don't fret about your opposition. Enemies of your writing always end up being good allies on your extended publicity team.

Here are a few of the many books on the American Library Association's challenged and banned list:

- *Ulysses* by James Joyce, selected by the Modern Library as the best novel of the twentieth century, was barred from the United States as obscene for fifteen years, and seized by U.S. Postal authorities in 1918 and 1930. The ban was lifted in 1933, only after advocates fought for the right to publish the book.

- *Leaves of Grass,* Walt Whitman's originally self-published signature collection of poetry, was withdrawn in Boston in 1881 after the district attorney threatened criminal prosecution for the use of explicit language. It was later published in Philadelphia.

- *The Rights of Man,* Thomas Paine's work defending the French Revolution, got the author indicted for treason in England in 1792. More than one English publisher was also prosecuted for printing *The Age of Reason,* where Paine argues for deism and against Christianity and atheism.

- *Lady Chatterley's Lover* by D. H. Lawrence—also originally self-published—was the object of numerous obscenity trials in both the United Kingdom and the United States as late as the 1960s.

- An illustrated edition of *Little Red Riding Hood* was banned in two California school districts in 1989. Following the Little Red-Cap story from *Grimm's Fairy Tales,* the book shows Little Red taking food and wine to her grandmother. The school districts cited concerns about the use of alcohol in the story.

- In Mark Twain's lifetime, *Tom Sawyer* and *Huckleberry Finn* were both excluded from the juvenile sections of libraries—including the Brooklyn Public Library—and banned from the library in Concord, Massachusetts, as "trash suitable only for the slums." In recent years, some high schools have dropped *Huckleberry Finn* from reading lists, or have been sued by parents who want the book dropped. In 1998 a parent's lawsuit that attempted to get a Tempe, Arizona, high school to remove the book from a required-reading list went as far as a federal appeals court.

- *Bless Me, Ultima,* Rudolfo Anaya's award-winning classic, was banned from the curriculum in Norwood High School in Colorado for offensive language.

- Judy Blume's books, including *Forever, Wifey,* and *Are You There God? It's Me, Margaret,* have earned the best-selling young-adult novelist the dubious title of "most banned writer in America."

Of course, we don't like censorship, but none of these challenges or bans seems to have damaged book sales. Not everyone is going to like your work. But if they really hate it—now, that's something to be proud of.

72 CHAMPION OTHER LIT STARS

It's easy to let writing and publishing and promotion become a cutthroat business. You get rejected by the same editor who just bought your student's manuscript. You compare advances with a colleague and come up short by six months' rent. You watch those fickle sales-rank numbers at Amazon.com rise and fall and you seethe: *My book is better than his!* It's easy to let your self-loathing self-importance carry the day. Don't take that easy road. Competition can be fun, but envy is pure poison. And there's something even more fun than competition: collaboration and mutual aid! Infighting may have plagued literary movements like the Harlem Renaissance, the "Lost Generation" of Left Bank writers, and the Beats, but truth told, not one of the famous authors who emerged from those movements would have had the same power without the community as a whole.

Writers write in isolation, but we all need a community when it comes to putting our work out into the world. Dexter Flowers hosts an open mic in my town, so I go out and share a story. Then I invite her to be my guest on a local community radio show and I promote her event. Michelle Tea hosts a monthly reading series at the San Francisco Public Library and invites me to come and read when my new book comes out. Kevin Sampsell tells me he's guest-editing an issue of *Spork* and I send him a short story by Adrian Shirk, a teenage student of mine, and she gets her first national byline. Annie Downey writes for *Hip Mama* and hosts me and my traveling brigade of book-tour performers when we're in Vermont. I read her fabulous book and offer a blurb. We plan a tour together. I organize events in town for authors passing through, write reviews, push to get them into the local media. I don't do it because I expect any favor in return or because I want to be a part of some old-friends' network, I do it because I believe in literature and envision a world where writers are supported, encouraged . . . treated like rock stars! It's a vision I'll vote for with my actions. It's a vision I depend on other lit stars to perpetuate. It's the opposite of arrogance. And it's plenty of fun.

73 TREAT THE WORLD AS YOUR OWN PERSONAL CLUBHOUSE

An Interview with Erika Lopez

Erika Lopez, the "half–Puerto Rican Quaker bisexual" author of four books, including *Flaming Iguanas* and *They Call Me Mad Dog*, hit the big time with big daddy Simon & Schuster back in the mid-1990s. She curled up on their big lap, took their big wallet, and toured the country, dining on rare filet mignon. She left big tips and even appeared on Tom Snyder's late-night show in a leopard velvet dress. After she misspent her fortune and ended up on the dole, she wrote and performed the world's first one-woman food-stamp variety show, *Nothing But the Smell: A Republican on Welfare*. Of course, Erika's not a Republican—she says she just has the rabid self-entitlement of one, a requirement for any lit star. But she insists she's too cool to be famous. And she might be right. While Erika's always happy to relieve a big publisher of a fat advance, when said fat advance isn't forthcoming, she takes matters into her own hands. The Queen of the Cross-Over, she's made a name for herself as a cartoonist, writer, publisher, performance artist, and now . . . hotshot producer!

Get all the dirt at monstergirlmovies.com.

WHEN DID YOU BECOME A WRITER?

Well, I've always been a cartoonist. I became a writer to make a living because cartooning at twenty-five dollars a pop just wasn't going to cut it. So I figured that I'd seen some really bad books—I could do that, too! All I needed was a little advance and I could figure out what to do after the money ran out. I couldn't keep a job, and well, my only other out was winning the lottery.

LIST YOUR ESSENTIALS OF MODERN PROSE.

I want to jar people, make them think, get angry, laugh, and give a damn.

HOW IMPORTANT IS PUBLICATION TO YOU?

The worst thing for an artist is being ignored. Publication improves your chances of not being ignored. Having art shows, doing graffiti, throwing a tantrum . . . In art school I used the Xerox machine like crazy and passed big magazines around and hung up posters for things that weren't happening and weren't ever going to happen. I self-publish all the time by making private little books and photo albums for myself or others.

WHAT'S THE MOST FUN YOU'VE HAD PROMOTING YOUR OWN WORK?

Promoting my *own* work and *fun?* That's more like throwing your baby kitten into oncoming traffic to see if it knows how to fly. So promoting my own work isn't so much fun. Unless I break it down with four shots of vodka. Then even realizing *I'm* actually the kitten isn't so bad.

All that I promote involves a severely split personality. You've gotta really pretend you're a crabby stage mom and agent, always hurling yourself into oncoming traffic to see if you really can fly. And the thing is, if you wave your scepters around enough, you actually *can* fly! Ha-ha!

But seriously, big daddy support from anyone can be nice, but I think if you treat the world like nothing more than your own clubhouse, you'll be surprised at what you can make happen. It's a whole new world, and sure, it's ugly, polarized between the broke-ass folks and their bosses, who've got four houses to themselves, but there's always a new way around an old problem of making a living, and sometimes you've gotta get your ideas from quiet history. Unknown facts. You can think you know too much and let it get you down, but the truth is that many artists and thinkers and writers have made livings with a little split personality shoving them out there. And so what if you embarrass yourself? I'm full of fear and embarrassment. Many of us are. But it's only boot camp for not giving a fuck later on, so use it to push on through the hardest parts of potentially making a fool out of yourself.

I'm not kidding. And I'm not competitive. I don't want to keep the secrets of a pretty successful artistic life to myself, because when I'm down, I desperately need to see other women, especially, doing something new and wrong and desperately needed in the world, and then I remember it's possible, and I get back up again.

If you don't have any outside inspiration, all this gets to be like drinking your own urine. Not very nourishing.

WHAT IS YOUR DEFINITION OF SUCCESS?

When I get letters from high-school kids who say that my books helped them feel kind of proud for being complete freaks in their schools. Yeah. That's the best. High school sucked for me and sometimes I just needed to remember that there *had* to be life after it, full of regular people like me.

DO YOU KNOW YOU'RE A GENIUS?

No, not a genius, but I'm pretty good at saying my own truth.

IS IT A DIFFERENT PROCESS WRITING WORK SPECIFICALLY FOR PERFORMANCE?

Yes, you have to be more concise and precise in performance. It takes actually performing it for me to learn what needs to come across in my body language or facial expressions, and how it might be redundant in my text.

HOW DO YOU ROLL WITH THE UPS AND DOWNS OF A WRITING CAREER? DO YOU EVER WISH YOU'D GONE INTO SOMETHING A LITTLE MORE STABLE, LIKE, SAY, GAMBLING?

If nothing's on the bigger horizon of a year or a few years, I get profoundly depressed. As long as there's the chance of a bigger score right around the corner, I'm okay. Just like a gambler, eh?

By the way, speaking of "eh," my first book, *Flaming Iguanas,* was about going cross-country on a motorcycle I barely knew how to ride ten years ago. I broke down and spent twenty-four hours with a couple of Canadian Johns and accidentally slept with the boring John and I wrote all about the night with them.

A few months ago, out of nowhere, I get a phone call from the other one and we talk all about that night and how pathetic I thought it all was. Now we have fallen in love. So whenever I hear or say "eh," I think of him. That's why I tell you this story.

WHAT'S ON THE HORIZON BESIDES LOVE?

I sold my rights to my one-woman food-stamp variety show to another crappy producer and realized that being broke and on the dole and schlepping my merchandise around and performing a show had taught me how to produce myself, so I decided to become my own hot-shot producer. Before I could talk myself out of it, I ran to city hall twenty minutes before it closed and registered my own business name, Monster Girl Movies. And so there it is. Now we've got a script for *Flaming Iguanas,* I've lost almost sixty pounds to play the lead myself, and some other producers actually want to work with me to make this happen.

Go figure.

So even if it only becomes a slide show, I'm having so much fun pretending I'm a hot shot to myself. Why should little kids be the only ones who get to march around naked, waving scepters in the air and demanding another glass of orange juice?

So there you have it. A creative life built on metaphors around scepters, kitties, orange juice, and urine. It all comes down to urine in the end, doesn't it? Remember, you don't have the kind of time to piss it all away.

Wishing you the best of luck in having it all!

ERIKA'S ASSIGNMENT

one-liners

Make up your own pithy quotes and pretend they're as important as ones by dead people that end up on bottle caps and gum wrappers.

74 ORGANIZE AN OUTRAGEOUS HEADLONG CROSS-COUNTRY TOUR

I always do like to be a lion, I like it again and again, and it is a peaceful thing to be one succeeding.

—**Gertrude Stein**

Step right up! Watch the continuing transformation of Ariel Gore!

See the Bay Area native turn her own single parenting into a growth industry, from zine to Web site to books to apparel, all bearing the unmistakable imprint of Hip Mama to the delight of her legions of fans. See the Portland resident turn her hopscotch, vagabond life into a well-regarded memoir.

Now watch Gore turn her latest book, *The Traveling Death and Resurrection Show*, into a West Coast book tour worthy of the novel's road-show subject. Author doing solitary lecturer turn at the mike? Forget it.

Gore is accompanied by musicians (Maria Fabulosa on bass, Nester Bucket on sax, Moe Bowstern on fiddle), plus a puppeteer. Plus, her obliging partner at the University Book Store, events maven Stesha Brandon, has lined up a couple of fire-eaters to set the mood outside the bookstore's entrance.

—*Seattle Post-Intelligencer*

Yea! I'm cruising down Highway 5 in a rented Toyota, my daughter and three performing friends along for the ride. I hate boring book readings! I want fanfare! So I've convinced Maria to play the bass, Nester to play the sax. The first press release promised Moe on the fiddle, so that's what it says in the paper, but she's got a trombone instead. My friends are more visually talented than I am, so they've made intricate shadow puppets to dramatize my novel. We wear thrift-store-snazzy circus-inspired pink and black. In bookstores and a few driveways down the West Coast, my fellow travelers play their instruments and run the puppet show while I read from my new book. More than a hundred people show up in Portland; fire artists join the show in Seattle; a stilt-walker livens things up in San Francisco.

What would be the point of all this writing and editing and rewriting and zine-making and book publishing and learning to talk if it didn't culminate in a rock-star-worthy tour? All for naught, if you ask me. And if you don't have a fancy publisher who'll send you out on a fancy tour, which might not end up being that much fun anyway because you have to stay in stiff-sheet hotels and you're not allowed to bring your friends, well then, you'll have to organize your own. It's easier than it sounds. Before you set out to plan a tour, I'm going to assume that you've planned a few open-mic or literary events in your hometown. You can do a basic reading and you can make a basic flyer, right? Now it's time to take your show on the road. It's best to tour with friends, so see if you can round up two or three fellow zine-makers or authors or musicians or clowns and get out a map. Where does each performer have friends or family who'll come out to hear you read? Make a few red dots on your map. Where—

between your red dots—are the university towns? Where are the cities famous for something related to what you write about? And where is the interstate? You're looking to draw a dotted line across some part of the nation with stops every fifty to three hundred miles. Don't try to drive more than three hundred miles a day.

An eleven-day West Coast tour, for example, might take you from Bellingham to San Diego by way of Seattle, Olympia, Portland, Eugene, Arcata, San Francisco, San Luis Obispo, and Los Angeles. Or maybe you're in Baltimore and you've got family in Montpelier. Short hops each day will take you through Washington, D.C., Philadelphia, New York, Providence, Amherst, Boston, and Portland, Maine. You'll want to focus on towns where you know somebody or you know of a good newspaper or bookstore, but a few blind in-between stops won't hurt you. An audience of three in Pismo Beach is still an audience. And sometimes it's actually easier to get people excited about a literary event in small towns that national writers tend to ignore.

Once you've mapped your trail, decide on some ideal dates. Give yourself five to eight months' lead time to organize the tour. Maybe everyone in your group can get two weeks off in April. Perfect. Most people are in town in April and the weather's usually passable. Start with your most important cities, pick up the phone, and see if you can book yourself some venues. You can find lists of independent bookstores online and you can find other friendly lit spots at letsdoitontheroad.com. While you're planning all this, why not give your tour an irresistible name? "The Wanderlust Tour" or "The Perpetual Motion Roadshow" is more likely to drum up interest than "Um, me and my friend wanna come read poetry at your store. . . ." Once you secure a few event bookings, build the rest of your itinerary around those. Start with bookstores, but don't ignore coffee shops, universities, magazine stands, bars, and, in a pinch, living rooms. It helps if you can give event coordinators some credentials—they may want a copy of your book or an e-mailed proposal. Mostly they want to know that you are going to bring in a few customers without doing something offensive. Lots of folks will say no. But someone will always say yes!

Once you've got your tour booked, it's time for some promo work. Make flyers and posters and send them to your venues, to libraries and cafés, and to any friends you have nearby. Send press releases to the big papers and the tiny zines in each town. Get yourself on the college radio show. Post announcements on the Internet. Invite the whole world! And before you head out, practice your readings and your show. You've put your all into planning this tour, so don't forget to plan your performances, too.

Save your pennies for gas and sandwiches. You can and should sell zines, books, and T-shirts and even pass a hat for donations at each stop, but don't count on making a ton of money on the road.

As the start date of your tour approaches, remind everyone to come out and see you, and when the sun comes up on the dawn of your first gig, get out on the road. You're a real lit star now!

75 STAND OUT ON THE CORNER IN A GORILLA MASK AND A PINK TUTU

My reading—scheduled months in advance in a dusty town twenty-five miles off the interstate—didn't get listed in the local newspaper. I was not invited to promote it on the local radio station. The bookstore events coordinator had, in fact, forgotten all about it. I knew no one in the state. So I put on a gorilla mask and a pink tutu and stood out on the corner passing out handbills I'd quickly photocopied at the town library. "This is a literary event you can't miss!" I cried.

That night, I read to a tiny rapt crowd of new fans. These folks had never heard of me, but here they were taking a chance on a crazy writer they saw out on the street because that crazy writer had taken a chance and approached them with her little handbill on the corner outside.

If it's in this book, it's been done before. But it's probably worth doing again. Go ahead! Put on your gorilla mask and your pink tutu! Odds are those marketing-saturated readers haven't seen anything like you, and the shock of the new will grab them. Surprise and delight. Pull them from their consumer daze and into the pages of your fine book.

"A writer who doesn't like personal attention should stick her nose into her work and never, ever feel she has to put on a monkey suit," Ursula K. Le Guin reminded us.

But a writer who wants folks to show up at her reading in that dusty town twenty-five miles off the interstate might do well to play the fool when she doesn't know anyone in the state.

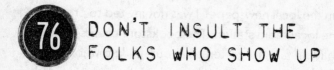

76 DON'T INSULT THE FOLKS WHO SHOW UP

I recently went out to a reading to hear a writer I'd always liked. She had a little punk-rock following, but I thought her work deserved more readers. This was her third book and I'd always wondered why she hadn't become more mainstream-popular. I would soon understand the problem.

About fifteen minutes after the reading was supposed to start, the writer stood up and moved her head back and forth as if she was checking out the crowd, but she didn't seem to make eye contact with anyone. She kind of sighed and shrugged at the same time. "I don't know if I should even bother reading," she finally whined. "This turnout is so pathetic."

My jaw dropped. I felt exactly the way I'd felt when I showed up at Wendy Smith's fourth-grade party, clutching the Hello Kitty stationery and pencil set I'd bought with my paper route tips, only to find her sobbing into her German chocolate cake: "Nobody came to my birthday party!"

Excuse me, but I came. Me and these five other people, we all showed up. *Pathetic turnout?* We rode our bicycles through the rain. We came out to support you. We are not nobody! But now we are going home and we think you're a jerk and you've just totally defeated the purpose of going on tour to begin with.

Now, I don't know if you've ever been to a business function where you were supposed to "network." I don't go to them myself. But I'm told you're supposed to get out there and "work a room." I understand that if you're going to go out there and have a psychotic episode instead, you're better off staying home. Going out on tour is like working the country. Sure, you'll have a mental breakdown in one or two towns along the way. You'll be tired and road-weary. You are totally entitled to your mental breakdowns. But when you get into that bookstore or café or bowling alley for your reading, I want you to look everyone in the eye who showed up and assume that they drove two hundred miles through a blizzard to come out and support you. You'd be surprised how many of them actually did. If you're having a mental breakdown, say, "I'm tired and road-weary and I'm having a mental breakdown, but I am so pleased to meet you."

Be gracious, for chrissake. No one had to be here but you.

77 SEND THANK-YOU NOTES

Look what I just got in the mail:

> Dear Ariel,
>
> Thank you for all your help, love, and support these past two years as I've been working on my book. Without your encouragement, it would have been a drag, and without your advice, I may never have gotten the thing published. You rock!
>
> Love,
> Jane

I'm not talking e-mail. This letter arrived in my real metal mailbox on my real wooden porch. A homemade card in an off-white envelope addressed by hand. How classy is that?

Everybody loves a thank-you note. *And to get one for a gift of support rather than anything tangible you can hold in your hand?* Amazing! If someone helps you with encouragement or logistics, send them a thank-you note. If someone lets you pirate their software to make your zine, send them a thank-you note. If someone puts you up when you blow through town on tour, send them a thank-you note. If someone feeds you while you're waiting for your advance, cheers you up when the bad reviews come out, or simply goes the extra mile to support your ass, send them a thank-you note. What your grandma taught you was right-on. When in doubt, send a thank-you note!

78 REMEMBER WHY YOU CAME HERE

A person who publishes a book appears willfully in the public eye with his pants down.

—Edna St. Vincent Millay

When my friend China Martens read that Edna St. Vincent Millay likened publishing a book to appearing publicly with one's pants down, she had an idea: "I'll put that quote on the poster for my book! And then I'll have a picture of myself with my pants down!"

I knew right then that China was destined to be a true literary star, and I told her so.

"Hmm," she said. "A famous writer? Does fame really matter? Isn't great writing what's important?"

Ugh, here was the question I'd hoped no one would ask while I was writing this book. The great "Who cares?" Maybe she'd even take it a step further and suggest that fame is in fact negative, corruptive, to be avoided.

"Of course fame is important," China went on, saving me from the dreaded reality that, at the end of the day, it isn't. "Having an audience and making money doing what you do—it's ideal. That and a good life now."

Can we just call her the Dalai China?

"Money and fame are mediums to be used like paint or steel or ideas," says Santa Fe arts writer Zane Fischer.

Fame is important and it isn't important. It's a language

of power, a muscle we flex so that we can make a living doing what we love. It's an illusion, both deliciously relative and cosmically fleeting. It exists as an energy between strangers; a magical agreement that we will support one another in our artistic leaps.

But don't let it go to your head.

Remember what Floyd Salas said when I asked him why he didn't give up after a few published writers kicked him in the teeth? He said, "First of all, I knew that I only meant good. I wasn't selfish."

All things are possible when you don't waste your power on selfishness.

And remember what Julia Alvarez said about staying flashproof? She was paraphrasing Spike Lee. She said, "The only way to be flashproof is to keep doing the work."

So when your day comes, and you burst onto the city like fireworks—your book in print and your name in lights—savor the moment.

And then go home and toast your real and good life now, and in the morning, get back to work.

So that's the advice I'm willing to give, Alli. Thanks for asking. I'm sorry it took me so long to respond; sorry that we didn't get a chance to work on your book together. But you know what China says? She says, "Fame after you're dead ain't so bad, either." Rest in peace, darlin'.

xo,
Ariel

ACKNOWLEDGMENTS

Thanks to Alli for asking me to be her mentor. And thanks to Jennifer Blowdryer, whose deliciously pompous advice-writing became infectious. Thanks to Amy Lee, Maria Fabulosa, and my agent, Faye Bender, who read the proposal and laughed (the encouraging kind of laugh, if I interpreted correctly). And thanks to my editors, Shana Drehs and Brandi Bowles, who took the project under their wings. Thanks to Inga Muscio for helping me with interviews and ideas. Thanks to all my students and the writers who posted lit star questions on my blog and livejournal. Thanks to China Martens and Tiffany Talbott, who edited early drafts of the manuscript and offered most-excellent feedback. Thanks to all the living famous writers who agreed to talk to me even if they were kind of suspicious about what I was up to, and thanks to Anaïs Nin and Gertrude Stein, who showed up in a black-and-white dream. Most of all, thanks to you, gentle reader: Thanks for picking up this book, and thanks in advance for telling all of your friends about me, because I'd really like to become a famous writer before I'm dead—I even quit smoking to give myself a few more years—and if you happen to know anyone at the *New York Times,* could you please tell them that I'm a genius? It would really help me out. In the meantime, take care, keep writing, keep fighting, and keep putting your work out into the world, okay? Surely we will meet someday.

ABOUT THE AUTHOR

The *Utne Reader* says: "Ariel Gore's transformation from globetrotting teenager to the hippest of mamas reads like a movie script about a Gen-X slacker following her bliss to unlikely success." She's the founder and editor of the award-winning parenting zine *Hip Mama,* and the author of five books, including *The Mother Trip, Atlas of the Human Heart,* and *The Traveling Death and Resurrection Show.* When she's not touring the country with a wondrous literary road show, she's teaching writing in Portland, Oregon. Click to arielgore.com for the latest.